Brain Injury and Returning to Employment

of related interest

Good Practice in Brain Injury Case Management
Edited by Jackie Parker
ISBN 1 84310 315 X

Children with Seizures
A Guide for Parents, Teachers, and Other Professionals
Martin L. Kutscher, MD
ISBN 1 84310 823 2

Music Therapy Methods in Neurorehabilitation
A Clinician's Manual
Felicity Baker and Jeanette Tamplin
With a contribution by Jeanette Kennelly
ISBN 1 84310 412 1

Stroke Survivor
A Personal Guide to Recovery
Andy McCann
ISBN 1 84310 410 5

Living with Brain Injury
Philip L. Fairclough
ISBN 1 84310 059 2

A Supported Employment Workbook
Using Individual Profiling and Job Matching
Steve Leach
ISBN 1 84310 052 5

Career Success of Disabled High-Flyers
Sonali Shah
ISBN 1 84310 208 0

Cracked
Recovering After Traumatic Brain Injury
Lynsey Calderwood
ISBN 1 84310 065 7

Brain Injury and Returning to Employment

A Guide for Practitioners

James Japp

Jessica Kingsley Publishers
London and Philadelphia

First published in 2005
by Jessica Kingsley Publishers
116 Pentonville Road
London N1 9JB, UK
and
400 Market Street, Suite 400
Philadelphia, PA 19106, USA
www.jkp.com

Copyright © James Japp 2005

Library of Congress Cataloging in Publication Data
Japp, James, 1962-
    Brain injury and returning to employment : a guide for practitioners / James Japp.
        p. ; cm.
    Includes bibliographical references and index.
    ISBN 1-84310-292-7 (pbk.)
    1. Brain damage--Patients--Rehabilitation. 2. Brain damage--Patients--Employment.
    [DNLM: 1. Brain Injuries--rehabilitation. 2. Occupational Therapy--methods. 3.
    Rehabilitation, Vocational. WL 354 J35b 2005] I. Title.
    RC387.5.J37 2005
    617.4'810443--dc22

                                                                    2004022995

British Library Cataloguing in Publication Data
A CIP catalogue record for this book is available from the British Library

ISBN-13: 978 1 84310 292 2
ISBN-10: 1 84310 292 7

Printed and Bound in Great Britain by
Athenaeum Press, Gateshead, Tyne and Wear

Contents

Acknowledgements

I would like to particularly thank the clients who helped me with various parts of this book. Having been through so much themselves they were only too happy to give up their time if it would help others going through the same process. Special thanks also to Kit Malia (Brain tree training) who provided fantastic guidance and support. Also to Hong-Lin Yu and Leslie Peters.

Preface

There has in recent years been a proliferation of literature on neurological impairment. However, it has been mostly confined to research or clinical issues and largely inaccessible to the increasing numbers of employment professionals now working with brain-injured people as part of a general remit. This book was written with a view to bridging the gap between medical provision for this group and the social and practical needs of returning brain-injured clients to the workplace.

This book is not academic in nature, nor is it theoretical. It does not contain models (accept as a means of explanation) or research. I have not striven to provide a balanced debate of all the issues but what works at a practical level. The idea behind the book is to provide a practitioner's perspective. The aim of the publication is to provide a practical overview of the problems that are likely to prevent a brain-injured individual from returning to work. It also looks at the environmental, emotional, physical, and psychological hurdles and barriers to work reintegration as well as solutions to some of these problems. It identifies occupational techniques that can be used to good effect.

The book is specifically related to acquired brain injury, where the injury is sustained in adulthood, where the neurological impairment is stable and possibly improving and the client is eager to return to employment following a period of absence. Neurological impairment is, however, a much broader field than acquired brain injury, covering developmental disorders as well as progressive conditions which have different implications for job skills and often call for different strategies in securing employment. To provide the reader with a greater understanding of brain injury, I have provided a broad framework of neurological impairment.

The term used to refer to an individual who has sustained an acquired brain injury varies according to the environment they are in and the source from which they were referred. It can include, among others descriptors, 'patient', 'client' or 'service user'. These terms are generally interchangeable but for clarity individuals will be referred to as 'clients' throughout this book. As the book cuts across professions, I have also considered an appropriate term to describe the staff working with the brain-injured individual, the typical reader of this book. 'Employment professional' seemed to be the most inclusive and relevant term.

Although my own professional background is in occupational psychology, the issues discussed in this book cut across professional remits. The book is aimed at the employment professional rather than brain injury expert. The reader will typically be a generalist working with all disability types but with a brain-injured caseload. It is aimed at the non-specialist practitioners working at the 'coal face' providing services to return brain-injured people to employment. The reader will come from such diverse professional backgrounds as occupational therapy, psychology, human resources, Connexion advisers, Jobcentreplus staff, social workers, job coaches, case managers and disability employment advisers. While the book was not written for client consumption, an individual with neurological impairment may benefit from its reading in terms of better understanding their condition and in gaining the confidence and knowledge to become active in their own rehabilitation and development.

Throughout the book I have endeavoured to develop a series of generalizations which provide a basis for the practitioner to form a framework, from which to get the best for their client. However, I do need to stress at an early stage that when it comes to brain injury, each person must be viewed as an individual.

Chapter 1

Introduction

Brain injury inevitably leads to time off work. Currently, the majority of moderately or severely injured clients do not return to work at the level enjoyed prior to their injury. Returning to work has enormous psychological connotations. It is the final hurdle to getting their life back and tangible evidence that progress is being achieved. Returning to work is a psychological boost to confidence. Having been out of employment through injury, most will have built up enormous financial liabilities in terms of mortgage repayments and loans and it is a relief to make any progress towards being able to repay some of the debts.

Until recently, brain injury has not been a priority of the statutory services and has not been well understood. A person who has lived with acquired brain injury for many years would not have had support following the acute stage of their recovery to enable them to return to employment. They were generally left to get on with it. Greater awareness coupled with increasing government funding has increased opportunities for vocational rehabilitation and support back into employment.

Survivors of brain injury were a lot fewer in number a generation or two ago. Historically, a person who acquired a debilitating brain injury would be employed on the land, farm labouring where their physical strength and some guidance from a colleague would be sufficient to help them through. Some managed to undertake these opportunities while others would depend on family support. In more recent years, individuals with brain injury would have worked in sheltered workshops which are basically factories employing disabled people. Most of this work was packing or basic low-skilled work such as assembly jobs. Government policy is now to integrate all disabled people into mainstream working environments. The Western world's shift away from an agricultural, industrial and manufacturing base to an information and service-based society has increased employment opportunities for disabled people in general, but individuals with cognitive deficits increasingly find it difficult to compete in this more complex employment market.

Severity of injury

When referring to acquired brain injury there are typically three levels of magnitude: mild, moderate and severe. The cognitive problems caused will be dependent on the seriousness of the injury and the particular part of the brain affected.

Mild brain injury brings with it subtle residues in cognitive deficit which often go unnoticed. Such an injury can be acquired from a small knock to the head through to a clash on the sports field or a whole host of other seemingly rather insignificant events, for which the individual concerned does not feel the need to seek medical intervention. The chances are that if they did seek medical opinion, it would remain unidentified. The person may experience a range of symptoms including: fatigue, depression, sleep loss, libido, concentration or memory impairment. It may also include an inability to concentrate when there is a lot of activity, increased irritability, inability to keep as much information as before in working memory or reduced processing speed. Although these can be minor, possibly unnoticeable problems, they have long-term consequences if the client, as often happens, feels they do not warrant further attention – particularly the cumulative negative effect on the person's workplace capabilities.

Symptoms are not usually permanent and pass in a relatively short duration. While a few months is a relatively short duration to live with a cognitive deficit, it is certainly sufficient time to lose a job. Furthermore, the method of losing the job can bring longer-lasting problems with finance and job references.

Moderate or severe brain injury can result in a whole host of unpredictable work-related problems which will have consequences for the individual's ability to undertake work tasks. As a generalization, unless there are severe physical disabilities, clients can generally undertake single tasks or tasks where there is an obvious sequence of events. It is dealing with multiple tasks simultaneously, or tasks requiring executive decision making such as prioritizing and negotiation, that brings the greatest difficulty.

By the time the employment specialist is involved, the client will have had experience of a wide range of therapeutic professionals. Some of that experience will be positive and some negative but this experience will inevitably colour how the client interacts with you. The successful vocational professional will identify and take steps to counter any pre-conceived ideas or fears at an early stage as well as identify established beliefs which need to be challenged and worked through. Paramount will be winning the client's trust. To undertake this successfully entails an understanding of all the issues and barriers that face the client as well as some appreciation of the journey they have taken before coming into your care.

Chapter 2

Neurological Impairment: The Broader Picture

The information contained within this book principally refers to clients returning to employment following an acquired brain injury. Nevertheless, it will be extremely useful to any employment professional involved in brain injury to have a broader understanding of neurological impairment and the type of issues that may affect an individual's ability to undertake their job. Consequently I have included such a framework. This will provide greater awareness of neurological conditions and the impact and potential barriers to employment from the varying conditions. It is designed to give the reader a framework for understanding of the issues involved and not meant as a framework to form the basis of your practice. Each client's particular needs are individual to them and it would be unacceptable to treat a client with neurological impairment in terms of group classification.

The brain's purpose

The enormous complexity of the world we inhabit means that more than any other species, humans are reliant on the predictable nature of their environment. Our actions and indeed thoughts are based on our experience of our world, and past reaction to our behaviour. The brain has many roles, but central to our ability to fit into society is the ability to create stable patterns for dealing with a stable world. The brain can be considered the 'go-between' connecting our inner and outer world. Damage to the brain blocks or distorts information received or supplied, resulting in chaos of communication and loss of the stable environment necessary for successful functioning in society.

The brain is often described as a high-functioning information processing unit, akin to a computer main frame. It is the decision centre of the human body, working on a variety of chemical impulses and chemical interaction. It weighs in the region of 1.5 kg and consists of a number of major structures. These include the *cerebellum* which helps co-ordinate fine motor movement. The cerebrum, which forms the greater mass, is made up of the right and the left hemispheres. The hemispheres are divided into four *lobes*: the frontal lobe, temporal lobe, parietal lobe and occipital lobe. Hundreds of millions of nerve fibres connect the two hemispheres through the *corpus callosum*, allowing communication between the two.

Categories of neurological impairment

In relation to employment, brain injury can be separated into five categories, although it has to be fully accepted that there are no absolute boundaries and a great deal of crossover between categories. The five broad areas are acquired brain injury, progressive neurological conditions, developmental/congenital conditions, neuropsychiatric conditions and viral/bacterial conditions. There is no medical basis for the framework I have formed. In developing this categorization, the main consideration has not been the nature or extent of the neurological impairment but the different needs in the workplace. It is based solely on the general requirements of employment and the consequences of neurological impairment to an individual's ability to undertake the day-to-day skills needed for their job.

The first principle considered in developing the categories within this framework is *acquired* as opposed to *congenital* brain injury. This is the distinction between growing up with neurological impairment from birth or acquiring impairment in adulthood. The second consideration is *stability*[1] versus probable *deterioration*. Some clients will acquire neurological impairment through illness or disease which is initially mild but will deteriorate. Others will acquire medium to severe neurological impairment but no deterioration is expected (in all likelihood they will improve). The third principle is *continuous* as opposed to *intermittent*. Certain clients have neurological impairment which is with them constantly or, in modern day parlance, they have it 24/7. For others, they have good periods when they function normally and bad periods when cognition is poor. This includes psychiatric conditions such as depression. The final consideration is a variation on the third principle, *permanent* as opposed to *transient* neurological problems.

Acquired brain (head) injury

An *acquired head injury*[2] can be caused by any traumatic insult to the brain either through external force or a weakness or disease within the brain itself. It is commonly caused by road traffic accidents, sporting incident, assault, stroke or a whole host of other methods. In this category, I would also consider a tumour to the brain or one-off invasive surgical intervention. However, a malignant tumour or any prospect of a recurrence of the initial disease would suggest that further deterioration is possible and employment prospects bleaker. This would be more likely to resemble a progressive neurological condition in terms of workplace support required.

There are a number of common themes which bind this as a category in relation to future employment prospects. Following a one off-injury to the brain, there will be a period of recovery and the individual will usually be left with residual cognitive problems, but it is unlikely that there will be deterioration unless further complications set in.

In this category, neurological impairment has occurred after the brain has fully developed.[3] Consequently clients will have lived relatively conventional lives up until the moment of their sustained injury. They will have high employment expectations, will be eager to return to their former employment and will need to go through a period of vocational rehabilitation. They will have families to support and have financial obligations to meet such as their mortgage and provision for their children. They may be carers to elderly parents. From this position of responsibility, they themselves become dependants and, in their own perception, a burden to their family. It can be a traumatic and painful reversal of roles for all concerned. Consequently there are specific emotional factors that need to be taken into consideration and worked through such as loss, anger, resentment, frustration, fear, self-loathing and worthlessness. The skilled vocational professional will usually have a good grounding in counselling, enabling them to support the client through difficult psychological adjustments.

There is a great deal of scope for development with this group and more requirement for support in this post-acute stage of recuperation to ensure that maximum recovery is achieved.

Progressive neurological conditions

A group that often calls for different supportive and intervention styles in relation to employment is clients with progressive neurological conditions. A progressive neurological condition is, of course, also an acquired disability. As far as the client is concerned, they acquired the disability in adulthood and lived a conventional life until doing so. Progressive neurological conditions include such illnesses as Parkinson's and Huntington's disease, as well as ataxia and multiple sclerosis. It is important to reiterate that there are no absolute boundaries and many individuals acquire these disabilities in a mild form with no further deterioration throughout their lifetime. This is particularly the case with multiple sclerosis, which takes a number of forms.

Of particular importance in categorizing this as a separate group in relation to employment needs is that solutions and adaptations that support the client in undertaking their job will need to be continually revised as deterioration in the condition occurs. Initially it calls for a minimal but continuous supportive plan, which is in place throughout the lifetime of the client. In all likelihood support will need to be increased as the client's condition deteriorates. This contrasts with the requirement of the one-off acquired brain injury where large amounts of resources are needed in the initial stages of returning the client to employment to maximize potential, but with a gradual reduction or complete withdrawal of the support as the client improves and maximizes their potential.

Although progressive illness can strike in relatively young people such as in Friedreich's ataxia, on the whole typical onset, or at least the symptoms of impairment impinging on work capabilities, is middle to later life, when retirement is more of an option or when the financial burdens and the need for achievement are not so great. Consequently employment can be less of a primary concern. This is certainly not to imply that employment is not important or attainable for this group. On the contrary, there is every evidence to suggest that active participation in work is necessary for the client's overall well-being. However, the purpose for employment or the incentives can be different and this may reflect how the employment professional approaches the management of the client.

Developmental/congenital brain injury

Congenital or developmental neurological brain injury is a birth or early childhood neurological defect. It includes a wide range of disabilities such as dyslexia, ADHD, cerebral palsy, Down syndrome, autism, epilepsy, Williams syndrome and general learning difficulty. For effective vocational intervention, each particular disability and its associated problems will need to be understood in its own right.

Intellectual and personal capabilities fluctuate enormously within this group. A great many will come into adulthood as normal functioning adults while others will have mild neurological impairment which will not adversely affect their ability to undertake their job. Some would very reasonably argue that their condition is an asset to them. There are many very able business people or successful artists with dyslexia or ADHD who struggled with the structured nature of formal education in childhood but come into their own when the more flexible world of employment enables them to utilize their own learning and interactive style. At the other end of the spectrum there is such severity of cognitive impairment and intellectual functioning that it will prohibit any form of employment, and independant living is the important goal to be achieved. Vocational professionals are likely to work with the middle range of clients with developmental neurological problems.

The first issue which binds this as a group is that acquiring neurological impairment in childhood can restrict or prevent the developing brain structures. This can result in global implications for functioning and intellectual abilities.

The second uniting element for this category is the psychological approach of the client. Individuals with acquired head injury have had their lives fundamentally altered and want to return to the point they were at prior to that disabling event. Clients with congenital neurological problems have lived with the disability all their lives, there has been no life change, it is part of them. For this group, particularly the more impaired, employment can be viewed as a frightening prospect in which it is someone else's ambition rather than their own. In the past, individuals with learning difficulty have often directly and indirectly had low expectation in terms of employment communicated to them. It is within my lifetime that individuals with the mildest of disabilities would have been placed in special schools and arguably occupied more than educated. For this group it is less about returning clients to previous work roles and more about increasing expectations and building confidence.

Neuropsychiatric disorders

Increasingly, the neurological consequences of some psychiatric conditions that impair cognitive functions are being recognized for their adverse impact on the individual's ability to sustain their job. This includes schizophrenia and severe depression. To understanding neuropsychiatric problems in relation to employment, two main groups can be formed: old age psychiatry and mental health.[4]

Old age psychiatry includes conditions such as Alzheimer's. This is principally (although not universally) a condition of old age which generally affects people who have entered retirement. Consequently it has minimal relevance for employment specialists. The condition is characterized by progressive cognitive deterioration including memory and concentration.

Mental health problems such as schizophrenia and depression are generally considered an acquired condition. Arguments exist over the acquisition of such conditions being genetic or environmental-based with, I suspect, most people concluding that it is a combination of both factors. The important issue is that the client generally becomes aware of their condition in adulthood and that they have lived conventional lives until the onset of the psychiatric condition which now afflicts their lives. Neurological problems can include poor concentration, difficulty with memory and poor decision-making ability.

The distinction drawn between the cognitive problems found in psychiatric conditions and that of other categories of neurological dysfunction discussed in this chapter is the intermittent nature of the problems. The neurological deficits in psychiatric conditions are very often transient in nature, with poor cognitive functioning in periods of illness which abates when there is a remission of the illness. There can also be a causal relationship between the medication that the client has been prescribed and cognitive ability. On some occasions medication will improve cognitive skill and on other occasions it will have an adverse impact.

The psychiatric client is more likely to need flexibility in their employment, to enable them to work when they are capable of doing so with the opportunity of time off when employment is either exasperating their condition or impacting too much on their ability to undertake their work duties.

Viral/bacterial infections

I have included as a separate group, impairment which derives from viral and bacterial infections (which I will call VBIs for ease of explanation), which can include such conditions as meningitis, CJD and AIDS. VBIs can occur in adulthood or in childhood. If it is acquired in childhood, there are likely to be developmental implications and consequently should be considered as such in relation to employment needs. The condition can be either stable or progressive. For example, the neurological damage[5] caused by meningitis can be severe, but once the infection is defeated, no further deterioration is expected and the disability can be managed as a stable condition. AIDS and CJD, however, are conditions in which neurological functioning (if affected) can progressively deteriorate until the individual's death.

I have included VBIs as a category on its own for two reasons. First, it does not sit comfortably within any other category. The second motive for a separate category is the nature of the impairment to the brain following infection, which is best illustrated by the rather gruesome but apt handgun/shotgun analogy. An acquired brain injury caused by external force (road traffic accident) or internal weakness to the brain (stroke) is akin to being shot by a handgun. The bulk of the damage is located where the impact of the single bullet penetrates. What occurs is massive damage to one area with a trickling effect to other areas. For example, a road traffic accident often involves major damage to the frontal lobes for the occupants of a car as the front part of the brain impacts with the skull.[6] This results in major dysfunction to the tasks controlled by that section of the brain (frontal lobe), namely executive functioning.

Viral infection is processed and distributed throughout the brain in the natural flows and ebbs of the brain's pathways. As a consequence, widespread distribution can cause more extensive but equal distribution of neurological damage. Like the effect of being blasted with a shotgun, it brings minor problems but over a much wider range. The combined consequences of the peppered shotgun effect can result in a worse outlook for the client and great difficulty to sustain employment. It is also more difficult to pinpoint the exact damage that has occurred without modern computer imaging such as a CAT or MRI scan.

Temporary impairment

There are many conditions that bring temporary neurological impairment which lasts for a few days or weeks and then recedes. This includes transient ischemic attacks and some types of damage by medication, alcohol or recreational drug use. Frightening as this is for the individual concerned, the condition is temporary and support and understanding from the employer and GP is beneficial until the individual has recovered function.

Notes

1 I refer to stability of cognitive functioning. There is every likelihood of psychological deterioration or at least fluctuation because of the enormity of the issues involved.

2 Brain injury and head injury are often used interchangeably to describe an acquired injury of this type. Head injury is reserved for an injury acquired traumatically as an adult, to distinguish it from the broader and more general concept of brain injury.

3 A one-off acquired brain injury sustained at some stage during childhood would likely have implications in the development of the brain and in most cases should be considered in relation to developmental brain injury.

4 In practice all psychiatric conditions come under the umbrella term of 'mental health'. This distinction is drawn for ease of clarification.

5 Not all viral or bacterial infections will result in neurological problems.

6 The brain, which is free-moving within the skull, is encased in a protective liquid. In a typical car accident, the body stops moving but the brain continues, impacting against the inside of the skull, causing shearing, bruising and bleeding and leading to cognitive damage to the frontal lobes of the brain.

Chapter 3

Acquired Brain (Head) Injury

As mentioned in the previous chapter, an acquired brain injury can be sustained by a variety of means including road traffic accident, as a consequence of assault, through a sporting injury or by internal sources such as a stroke or tumour. Most people who acquire brain injury are likely to be young men of working age between 17 and 30. This is much to do with their lifestyle. They have less driving experience, are more likely to drive fast and dangerously and not to take safety precautions. Consequently they are more likely to be injured in a car accident. They are more likely to become caught up in violent confrontation. They are more likely to indulge in recreational drug use and more likely to work in a dangerous environment such as a building site or industrial factory.

The consequence of severe injury can be complex and chronic leading to lifelong disability. Some clients need to relearn virtually everything from scratch. It often means a barrage of change for the individual and, on many occasions, a complete transformation of their personal and social lives. Each individual will have unique experiences in their journey subsequent to their acquired injury. It will be a journey of months if not years of rehabilitation, hope, despair, some triumphs and a great deal of personal readjustment. Gaining employment is often viewed as the final hurdle.

Neurological impairment is an invisible injury so it is not given the same understanding or support as a physical injury. For most people, including employers, if they cannot see a disability they assume that one does not exist. This can be one of the most frustrating aspects of a brain injury for the client because others do not understand their situation, expecting as high standards from them as they would of a non-brain-injured person.

The journey

At the acute stage of the client's recovery, resources are concentrated on medical stability and the fundamentals such as relearning motor movements, speech and independent living. Individuals who acquire a brain injury will usually have been measured on the *Glasgow Coma Scale*.[1] The extent of possible brain injury can also be gauged by neuro-imaging techniques such as CT scan and MRI scan and neurophysiologic assessment techniques such as the electroencephalogram (EEG).

Many if not most of the clients will have no memory of how they sustained their injury, particularly in the more serious cases or where the injury occurred through a traumatic blow to the head.[2] The individual involved in the trauma will come to consciousness some weeks following their injury, hazy from medication and weak from the strain of medical intervention, with little recollection of the event. Often they will have no memory of the first few weeks and months in hospital and no memory of a sizeable period before the actual injury itself. Typically, they will describe a feeling of 'un-realness', of witnessing events but being unable to respond to them. When they are relaying to you the background to their injury, they are invariably piecing it together from what they have learned from the medical profession and from their family and friends.

One can only imagine the alienation, fear and aloneness of these first weeks of semi-consciousness in hospital. Initially they may not recognize family members or close friends. They can be confused, not knowing where they are or how they got there. They are in a world full of strangers and unfamiliar contraptions of which their damaged brain will continue to try and make sense. Often they are in pain from other injuries, although I am told that this can be a blessing as it detracts from the anxiety of their unfamiliar environment. They have never experienced this situation before and having no concept of a brain injury or the problems caused by it, can have no understanding of the circumstances in which they find themselves.

The process of rehabilitation for the brain-injured client starts immediately. Most recovery is made in the first six months to one year, although there will be opportunity for further improvement over a number of years. The acute stage may involve physiotherapy input, restoring everyday functions such as bowel control and feeding. Acute rehabilitation will involve ensuring the client is back on their feet walking, improving their balance, co-ordination, improving stamina, increasing dexterity and strength. They may also work with a cognitive rehabilitation therapist to improve cognitive functioning or a neuropsychologist to resolve inappropriate behaviour. A speech and language therapist may work on the client's communication if necessary. Release from hospital will involve becoming an outpatient and the intermediate care team taking over. Intermediate care involves assessing and supporting the client's ability to live at home, shopping, cooking, tidying up, dressing etc. The severely disabled individual may be taken into long-term residential care if circumstances prevent them from returning home.

For clients likely to be awarded compensation for their injury, the process will be longer and there will be additional involvement with medical and vocational professionals. This further consultation will be under the instruction of the defence legal team and the claimant legal team, both seeking to establish the extent of the injury and the potential financial loss to the client, enabling them to identify the appropriate amount of reparation. Few take this in their stride and most are quite understandably drained by it all.

A fragile existence

A further blow to a fragile sense of self for individuals who have acquired cognitive problems following brain injury is that friendships often evaporate. Parents and spouses view the loss of their loved one's friendships as one of the most painful parts of the whole process for them. In the initial stages, friends are there for support but as the long-term nature of the injury becomes apparent and it is obvious the person has changed in some ways, friendships can wither on the vine. When these are gone, it leaves the client empty, embittered and isolated. Friendships dissolve for many reasons. Some fade because neither party is sure where they stand. Often it is the acquired brain-injured client who shows no interest. Such a long period can elapse between acquiring the injury and the client feeling ready to pick up their relationships that it is difficult for them to reactivate them. Behavioural problems coupled with financial hardship can also cause marriage break-ups and family alienation. Support mechanisms evaporate and the client descends into depths they never thought imaginable.

It is against this background that the employment professional becomes involved, working with the client to stop the downward spiral and supporting the client as they slowly climb their way back up. Working with brain-injured clients will teach you how fragile our existence really is but also how remarkable is the human capacity to triumph over adversity and to evolve in new directions.

Notes

1 It is worth having a working understanding of the Glasgow Coma Scale as you are likely to read about it in various reports on your client. It is an instrument devised in 1974 by Teasdale and Jennett to determine a patient's observable responses to outside activity. It is a method of detailing conscious and subconscious motor and verbal responses. Patients (as they would be then called by the medical profession) would obtain a score between 3 and 15, 15 being a person who is fully orientated in time and space. This scale can be used as a rule of thumb as to the possible severity of the brain injury. A score of 8 and under is indicative of severe head injury, a score of 9 to 12 a moderate head injury and above 12 indicates a mild head injury.

2 Individuals who have sustained brain injury through internal causes such as a stroke or weakness to a blood vessel in the brain often have a complete memory of the event. Perhaps this is related to the speed at which the damage occurs, with a stroke probably taking quite a few minutes to cause damage as opposed to the sudden impact of an external blow to the head.

4

Brain Injury Problems

No two clients with an acquired brain injury will present with the same disabilities. A memory problem will affect different people in different ways, as will deficits in concentration or other areas of cognition. Consequently it is essential that the unique characteristics prohibiting the individual from gaining employment are understood. While the extent of disability is generally commensurate with the severity of the injury, seemingly trivial trauma to the head can result in serious cognitive problems while severe trauma including significant loss of part of the brain can at times produce relatively mild impairment. Symptoms of brain injury can also be greatly exaggerated by psychological factors such as anxiety or low confidence. Some loss of ability following cognitive impairment is obvious while others are subtle, unobservable and not measurable or detectable by clinical assessment.

This section is intended to give the reader an awareness of some of the more common and obvious problems associated with an acquired brain injury. However, it is not a complete picture. There are many other aspects of cognition affected by brain injury not detailed here including: smell, taste, motivation, depression, mental health, acquired dyslexia and visual neglect, to name a few. The cognitive deficits in isolation are themselves massive barriers to employment but the greatest difficulty prohibiting a return to employment lies in the combination of problems: the cognitive deficit combined with physical injury, behavioural issues and the affective state. Successful reintegration into employment depends on understanding these areas as well as the interplay and dynamics between them.

Memory

The human memory structure is extremely diverse and dispersed throughout the brain. Consequently there is more opportunity for injury to this function. Memory, processing speed and attentional problems are the most frequently cited cognitive complaints following acquired brain injury. Many academic theories and models exist to explain memory structure. Categories of memory depend very much on the particular field of expertise involved with the client but can include declarative, sensory, global, specific, procedural, episodic, semantic, explicit, implicit, long- term, sensory, short-term, retrograde, anterograde, verbal, visual, spatial and a whole host of other areas.

Employment professionals assisting brain-injured people back to employment are not usually expected to be specialists in memory or any other cognitive area, and can realistically only aspire to have a broad but basic understanding of cognitive issues. In relation to memory, I propose the areas detailed below to be the most necessary for employment. This approach is oversimplified but it is intended to bring clarity when bridging the gap between a multidisciplinary medical team and a client's employers, enabling a transition from a medical setting to a work setting.

In order for an employee to understand workplace instructions and carry out everyday job duties, they must be able to retain instructions and information in their *working memory* for a sufficient time in order to commit to memory the nature of the task required. Working memory is described as information that can be held in conscious memory and used or worked with at that time. An example is remembering a telephone number just given to you. Information is remembered in a number of ways: through *verbal memory* which is spoken or written information; through *visual memory* which is information gained through visual senses; and through *spatial memory* which is a memory of the layout of objects. Good memory is dependent upon using verbal, visual and spatial memory simultaneously.

Similarly, to undertake a task on an ongoing basis, there needs to be a degree of continuity to memory, to enable tasks to be undertaken over a period of time, without having to be reinstructed on a daily basis. This is a *medium-term memory* requirement.

Other aspects of memory are, of course, important to everyday functioning, but it is the ability to remember in the 'here and now' that is the vital component in terms of returning to the workplace. What an individual can recall from their past, *long-term memory*, will be very important to them personally, but it has a lower priority in relation to returning to work, as it will not always directly affect their work performance. Should a graduate or professional be unable to recall their training (long-term memory, procedural memory, etc.), it affects their future career, but for immediate employment rehabilitation, they are likely to be undertaking fairly low level non-professional duties. Inability to remember professional information will surface as the client assimilates back into the workplace and attempts to progress to their previous duties.

Retrograde amnesia refers to the loss of memory prior to injury. The extent of retrograde memory loss can be used by the medical profession as a general measure of the severity of the injury and prospect of recovery. Retrograde amnesia can vary from a few minutes or hours in terms of memory loss, but can also be months or, in extreme cases, years. A few clients will have no memories from before their accident. They are unable to recall educational qualification, childhood friends, birthdays, Christmas etc. Extensive retrograde amnesia often correlates with difficulties in laying down new memories. However, if clients are able to form new memories, there is nothing preventing them from succeeding in employment, although it remains unlikely that they will return to their previous job.

Although prior memories cannot be restored if organic brain injury has occurred, a cognitive rehabilitation therapy programme can be incorporated to relearn essential memories where possible. This involves setting information-gathering exercises for the individual to relearn their personal biographical history.

Post-traumatic amnesia describes the inability to recall events that occurred after the injury was sustained. The extent of this can be more

difficult to establish because of the impact that sedation has on consciousness. Sedatives are commonly used in the acute phase of recovery,
to support recovery or if the client goes through a period of aggression,
which can occur. Generally for severe head injured clients, the first few
months following injury can be lost or, in the most severe cases, up to
the first year.

Confabulation is where the client provides wrong information when
they cannot remember the factual truth. It usually occurs because clients
sense that they should know the information requested and are embarrassed that they do not. It is not a wilful attempt to deceive or to gain
advantage. It can be difficult to detect confabulation as clients can be
quite convincing and confident in relaying this false information.

As a general rule, if memory impairment is severe, the individual is
unlikely to be at the stage of seeking employment. The typical client
group seeking employment will have mild to moderate memory
problems (usually verbal) and this prevents them from learning new
information as quickly as commercial organizations expect. This is why
appropriate support is needed in returning the individual to the employment market.

Sometimes it is possible to identify the likely work-related issues
encountered by an individual. With memory problems difficulties will
relate to the actual memory deficit which may be verbal, visual or spatial
in nature. With a reduction to verbal memory capacity, a client will
struggle learning new tasks and only be able to undertake novel tasks
where the requirements are low skilled and self-evident, or where there
is visual demonstration and continual reinforcement until a set pattern
has been established. Difficulty remembering appointments, passing on
information or remembering a customer's name, have obvious implications for successful work performance.

Attention

Attention and concentration are often used interchangeably but strictly
speaking concentration is one aspect of attention. Inability to concentrate for prolonged periods, or being easily distracted by ongoing
activity, is often associated with frontal lobe damage. Poor concentra-

tion reduces the client's ability to work productively, to sustain a job or to learn new tasks. It can lead to frustration, anger and general feelings of hopelessness. Attention/concentration deficit is not a unitary defined concept but a combination of different events culminating in a sluggishness or inability to process cognitive information. Although a common problem with acquired brain injury, attentional problems improve more than most other cognitive areas, through natural spontaneous recovery and by work rehabilitation.

Sustained attention is the ability to concentrate for prolonged periods. This can be defined as about a 20-minute period or more. It is easy to understand how poor sustained attention is likely to impinge on work duties that require the client to concentrate for longer periods. The client with sustained attention difficulty is unable to concentrate for a long enough period to complete tasks. They may be able to undertake the task for a short duration but soon become confused, resulting in error in their work performance. Routine and monotonous tasks can be equally if not more difficult as complex tasks to complete.

Divided attention is the ability to deal with competing information. The more complex a job, the more probability of inability to divide attention between different activities becoming an issue. Despite the old idiom that we cannot do two things at once, we very often do, particularly in work situations. For example, a driver can listen to the radio but at the same time be visually alert for signs of danger while driving. A receptionist will listen to a telephone message at the same time as scribbling down the details being communicated. This ability is lost in clients with poor divided attention, who cannot deal appropriately with competing information. They cannot listen to instructions while at the same time assimilating the contents of the instructions into comprehension.

Selective attention is the ability to pick out appropriate information and filter out irrelevant information. Often a client can focus on single tasks well and complete tasks at a commercial speed. However, poor selective attention results in inability to multitask or to undertake a number of tasks simultaneously. It reduces the person's ability to select what is irrelevant and which details are most important to attend to.

When returning to employment, a gradual build-up of tasks combined with frequent rest periods can help to reduce problems of attention. Health and safety issues such as working with machinery, working with chemicals or working at heights need to be taken into serious consideration when attention is adversely affected, both for the client's safety and that of their colleagues. Appropriate steps can be taken to change the environment wherever possible.

Poor *speed of information processing* is one of the major problems with successful vocational reintegration and unfortunately one of the most common problems following acquired brain injury. Slower processing speed has a knock-on effect in other cognitive capabilities such as working memory and executive skills.

Often the individual will need to consciously process the information before comprehension is attained, where prior to injury the process was automatic and undertaken at a subconscious level. Consequently they may be inclined to respond slower than most and additional time needs to be built in to the task to compensate.

Executive functioning

Executive function is best described as the decision-making process of the brain and in particular is involved in planning and initiating. A good analogy of executive functioning is of the executive in a company making decisions and all the processes that this would involve. Although the term 'executive decision making' sounds impressive, all employees undertake this activity as a matter of routine. A truck driver views an event on the road ahead of them and undertakes a calculation at a subconscious level as to the best course of action. This is an executive decision. A poor 'executive choice' may well lead to an accident resulting in injury or their death. Executive skill entails mostly frontal lobe functioning although ability for this skill resides throughout the brain.

Damage to executive functioning can result in poor decision-making skill, poor attention, increased distractibility, poor long-range planning, difficulty in organizing, difficulty changing established rules, poor judgement and poor self-monitoring. Clients with executive problems can have particular difficulty dealing with ambiguity and can be confused in situations where there is no right or wrong solution but where the resolution of the problem lies in the individual's own judgement. Difficulty with executive functioning may cause the person to respond inappropriately or to lose track of the task at hand. They can also have great difficulty adapting to novel situations. Individuals with executive damage can lack initiative and spontaneity. They can have difficulty switching from one task to another or copying text from one book to another. They quite naturally adopt a rigid devotion to routine as the familiarity of a task helps them to cope.

Executive functioning is also dependent on memory and concentration to a large extent. If an individual cannot concentrate on the instruction or cannot retain the information in their head, executive ability will be deprived of its main source of 'energy'. It can, at times, be difficult to ascertain if it is memory/concentration deficits that are impinging on executive skills or vice versa.

It is easy to understand the likely difficulties that might arise if this type of ability is adversely affected. Poor executive decision making can lead to difficulty in prioritizing and analyzing data. Prioritizing the most important tasks, to ensure precedence over less essential duties, is a vital aspect of successful employment. Poor analytical skills may indicate difficulty using information to predict or generate new information based on past data. With difficulty prioritizing and analyzing, clients with no previous work-related experience to fall back on would need support when changing job duties. In relation to employment, the more complex and varied the work tasks involved in their job, the more that poor executive functioning will be a problem in returning to employment.

Speech

Inability to articulate thoughts into productive speech is not only immensely frustrating for the individuals concerned, but in the modern workforce there are few jobs an individual with a speech deficit can undertake. Despite the client's poor speech production, they are usually more able to understand speech than they are to produce it, which increases their levels of frustration.

Speech difficulties encountered by brain-injured clients include word finding, perseveration, rambling in conversation, not always sticking to the story, poor turn-taking skills, poor speech projection, delays before responding, difficulty sustaining the conversation and inability to use appropriate facial gestures. Circumlocution can be used by some individuals because they cannot find the word they are trying to express, consequently will use other words to describe what they wish to communicate. Some will produce a related but incorrect word: for example, 'two' when they mean 'five' or 'March' when they mean 'June', and 'yes' when they mean 'no'.

When conversing with another person, there are natural signs and indications for turn taking in conversation which oil the wheels of communication. This process is at a subconscious level. Individuals with acquired brain injury may not provide or comprehend the normal cues and breaks for two-way communication during conversation. There may be difficulty interjecting when in conversation with them. Consequently social communication and relationship building can break down.

Literacy and numeric skill

Literacy and numeric skill can be damaged as a consequence of an acquired brain injury. Included in this is the physical ability of holding and writing with an instrument. Some of the difficulty may be attributed to brain damage affecting motor movement. Skills affected can be both varied and multiple, including the inability to read, write or the substitution or omission of words. Some will have a tendency to write very small letters, caused perhaps by needing greater control of the writing instrument. They may be capable of writing a word down but unable to read it back. *Agraphia* refers to the loss of ability to express ideas in written form. *Alexia* refers to word blindness. Traumatic brain injury can also result in an acquired dyslexia.

Inability to deal with numbers is called *acalculia*. *Anarithmetria* is the inability to perform number manipulations although numerical skills remain relatively intact. Both these disabilities can be found in brain-injured clients although relatively rare. Individuals who have not attended formal education for many years – the majority of the population – often forget the rules of calculation. This is not the same as organic cognitive damage to the skill base. Numeric capability is generally less affected than reading and writing which can probably be attributed to the structure of reading and writing being based widely within the brain, giving more opportunity for damage to this skill.

Poor written communication skills or inability to deal with numbers will adversely affect employment options. As with speech, it is difficult to think of many jobs an individual can undertake in the modern workforce without adequate ability to read and to write or to count. Basic packing jobs require an ability to count widgets into a box.

Behavioural problems

Injury to the brain can cause behavioural/emotional-related problems, particularly disinhibitions. The person is unable to regulate their behaviour in the way that they could prior to their head injury. On occasion, there is a complete reversal of personality. Outgoing people become reserved and vice versa. More common is an exaggeration of previous tendencies that were already traits of the individual. For example, a tendency to perfectionism, which may have been endearing prior to injury, is over-emphasized to the point that nothing is ever achieved. Overaccuracy in working with a task to the detriment of speed is a common exaggerated tendency with predictable detrimental outcomes in work performance. Some individuals will become obsessive, for example compulsively tidying. On other occasions clients may employ more levity and humour than pre-injury personality, but often inappropriately applied. This could be a result of misjudging the occasion or as means of deflecting attention from their other difficulties. Emotional ups and downs can also be evident, particularly with more recent head-injured clients.

Often individuals with acquired brain-injury will have difficulty controlling anger. While they do have a lot more to be angry about, they can become irritated over relatively trivial matters. They have great difficulty dealing with the workplace conflict inevitable in any job. Conversely, a client can sometimes be too compliant and laid back – nothing seems to bother them. Their laid-back approach can be mistaken for apathy or disinterest in their work duties.

Interpersonal relationships are essential to success in the workplace. The brain-injured employee can be impervious to the non-verbal cues that their behaviour is unsuitable, which the rest of us pick up at a sub-conscious level. Socially unacceptable behaviour has obvious implications for workplace acceptance and success of the client in their return to employment. Asking inappropriate information of a sexual nature, poor judgement when revealing information about themselves to others, or not screening in any way their feeling or thoughts before relaying information to colleagues, are potential issues. While no malice is intended on the part of the brain-injured client, their actions will cause colleagues to feel threatened or embarrassed. Employers are responsible for providing a safe environment for all their employees. Few employers will retain a brain-injured person who is potentially going to make other staff members feel uncomfortable or threatened.

Interactive skills

Success in today's employment market is related to interpersonal skills as much as it is to IQ level. Establishing and maintaining social contact calls on higher cognitive skill and is of particular concern in acquired brain injury. As mentioned previously, dwindling friendships in personal and home settings are commonplace but are often of little concern to the client. Nevertheless they can be a concern for the parents of a brain-injured teenager, for a spouse or indeed for an employer who is reliant on a team approach in the workplace.

There is no reason why friendships need to disintegrate at the very time when they are critical to the client's reintegration into the work and their overall sense of self. It is important to understand the reason behind the difficulty in maintaining peer friendship.

A number of common themes have been suggested for the client's unwillingness to continue with workplace friendships but this is only the tip of the iceberg and if this is an issue for your client, it should be explored thoroughly with them. Justifications have included that their friends' career success serves as a guide to how successful they themselves would probably have been, if the accident had not occurred. Alternatively they now have less in common with friends/colleagues from the past. More likely is the view that they may be embarrassed about their situation and reduced abilities, so avoid contact.

Vision

Visual problems occur (relatively frequently) as a consequence of a brain injury, either through damage to the optic nerve, optic chasm, optic tract or visual cortex. While loss of vision can be a consequence of structural damage to the brain, in some circumstances the brain will receive information from the visual senses, but cannot recognize the information being presented to it.

Typical visual problems include visual blindness, blind spots, visual neglect and double vision. Damage to the optic nerve may result in loss of visual acuity whereas damage to the optic pathways in the occipital lobes or the temporal lobes will cause *diplopia* or eye movement disorders. Some minor visual problems can be easily compensated for by the use of correct equipment in the workplace or by the use of spectacles by the client.

Insight

Insight, in lay terms, refers to awareness of our abilities/inabilities, particularly in relation to the changes brought about by injury. Areas of the brain involved in awareness include the limbic region, temporal lobes and frontal lobes. Our experiences as we go through life generally lead us to form a subconscious awareness of our capabilities. New experiences will perhaps change our perceptions of this ability in one direction or another but traumatic brain injury often seriously impairs our cognitive skill without a corresponding devaluation of our ability in self-awareness. In short, the individual believes they have the same ability that they had prior to their injury, despite the overwhelming evidence to the contrary.

Our level of insight into ourselves will fluctuate from one part of our lives to another. What is important is that awareness or insight is sufficient for us to function effectively in society. Reduced insight usually suggests that the client has little awareness of the consequences and extent of their injury and disability. Often they are more optimistic about their future than their family or the rehabilitation staff that are supporting them. Family and friends may think the person's ability has deteriorated while they themselves view their behaviour/cognitive functioning to be similar to pre-injury levels. If an individual does not understand their limitations or their capabilities, or how others are reacting to their behaviour and demeanour, progress in the workplace can be prohibited.

Orthopaedic injury

Cognitive injury is often accompanied by physical injuries. Orthopaedic injury can be a consequence of damage to the actual muscular/skeletal site which can be classed as a mechanical injury or to that part of the brain which controls the body part affected. Orthopaedic injury can vary in intensity from slight impairment of control to no control. Reduced motor control of the legs, back, arms or indeed any part of the skeletal structure can occur.

Related difficulties can include poor hand-eye co-ordination, difficulty with balance, poor bilateral symmetry and poor proprioception. Injury to the cerebellum will affect fine co-ordination of muscles, causing difficulty to stand and to walk, and therefore leading to clumsy movement. If the motor cortex is damaged, it will affect motor movement.

Left hemispheric damage will adversely affect motor control to the right side of the body and vice versa. One side of the body may function normally while there is little or no function to the other. Clients often describe having no feeling to the affected part of the body although being conscious (if not overconscious) of physical limitations. In relation to employment, poor dexterity will affect speed and accuracy of performance, reducing the individual's ability to work at a commercial level.

Pain

Cognitive damage creates a great deal of frustration and anger but no physical pain although the consequences of neurological impairment such as reduced concentration can directly cause headaches. Although not strictly a deficit in performance, pain can impinge on cognitive functioning and reduce an individual's ability to undertake their job. Therefore pain experienced should be a factor for consideration when returning a brain-injured individual to employment. Acute pain is the pain felt after the body has received an injury and at its simplest is described as the body's warning system. This can be contrasted with chronic pain which is long term. Chronic pain usually comes from orthopaedic injuries sustained in the same accident. Specialists in pain management view pain as a highly subjective phenomenon. What one person finds tolerable, others may find unbearable and this should be a consideration to the practitioner supporting an individual who incures a degree of pain. Pain can also be amplified by personal, emotional or situational factors such as stress.

Pain can have a number of consequences in relation to work performance. It can adversely affect concentration and attention, which then lowers performance in other areas and increases health and safety risks. Pain can also influence motivation, where the individual's energy is drained by focusing on their pain and how to ease it, rather than focusing on returning to employment and increasing their work-related skill.

Pain relief comes from a variety of sources. Medication has two main formats. Non-prescribed medication for mild pain includes aspirin. Prescribed medication is often opiate in nature. Opiates derive from opium and operate by depressing central nervous processing. Morphine is probably the most well known opiate. Some of the side effects of prescribed medication, including drowsiness and reduced concentration, can also adversely impact on cognitive performance in the workplace.

There are increasing numbers of chronic pain specialists working with long-term sufferers of pain. Individuals who experience chronic pain will usually have tried a number of pain management interventions, which can include acupuncture, massaging the pain site, electrical stimulation, ice pack or selective exercise. Work activity in which the brain is distracted can be an effective method of pain relief. Appropriate seating and ergonomically designed workstation can help to minimize pain and its impact on workplace performance.

Final thoughts

Clients with serious multiple injuries frequently explain only their more severe residual disabilities, overlooking what they may view as minor distractions such as deafness, epilepsy or visual impairment. These may seem relatively unimportant to them, given the severity of other conditions, but can be instrumental in successful workplace reintegration. From a health and safety perspective as well as being able to identify an appropriate workplacement, it is essential to obtain information on all potential restrictions in the workplace.

Chapter 5

Vocational Assessment

As an employment specialist involved in supporting a brain-injured individual, you will be required to take decisions in relation to placing the client at the appropriate level, in a suitable work environment. To undertake this successfully requires identifying the individual's workplace capabilities. Establishing abilities, competence and post-injury employment ambitions generally comes under the term 'assessment'. The extent to which you will be able to formally assess a brain-injured person will largely depend on your own professional background and the depth of your training in assessment methods.

Ideally, the client referred to you will have undertaken a specialist neurological assessment and have sufficient specialist support, which can be passed on from the rehabilitation unit to the employer or employment professional. In practice, however, this is highly unlikely and you will be required to undertake some judgement and identification of the person's cognitive capabilities, although I stress you should not be making diagnostic assessments of cognitive capabilities unless competent to do so.

Cognitive assessment

The cognitive assessment[1] of brain injury is a specialist activity which will usually be undertaken by an occupational psychologist, neuropsychologist, occupational therapist or by a specialist cognitive rehabilitation therapist. A typical assessment will consist of a battery of tests which aim to assess the extent of behavioural and cognitive problems of the kind outlined in the previous chapter. As well as administering a number of clinical tests, the specialist cognitive assessor will observe everyday behaviour of the client, how they engage in everyday tasks and their ability to function in society. They will have discussed pre-injury/post-injury behaviour with the client and their family. Part of their remit may be the identification of psychological issues such as mood and depression as well as the effect of medication which can cause or exaggerate cognitive deficiency. This type of holistic overview will enable the cognitive specialist to obtain an accurate overview of the person's cognitive capabilities.

The cognitive assessments that are available from specialists do not always assist the employment professional. A client's performance in controlled clinical environments of the kind in which such assessments are undertaken, will not generally transfer to the more complex work situations which require intuition, dealing with novel situations and undertaking a number of tasks simultaneously. It can be the case that a person performs within the normal range in the relaxed atmosphere of an assessment room, but has more difficulty when faced with the complexity of a working environment. Cognitive skills are at their poorest immediately following injury, with cognitive ability improving thereafter. Consequently the information contained within such a report can quickly become dated, particularly if the individual was assessed shortly after the acquisition of their injury, when natural spontaneous recovery of brain function has yet to be maximised.

A full neuropsychological assessment conducted by a neuropsychologist can be expensive and specialists who provide them are scarce, so not all individuals who have acquired a brain injury will have gone through this process. Of those who have undertaken a neuropsychological assessment, there can often be a reluctance to pass on the information due to the confidentiality issues involved. Consequently, despite a specialist assessment report being available, an employment professional may not gain access to this information. Neuropsychological assessments principally establish the type and level of brain dysfunction that the client has incurred, but are not always informative on providing advice on returning the client to work at the appropriate level.

Informal observation

The employment professional should proactively identify in what way the cognitive problems of their client will affect ability to undertake workplace tasks, prior to placing them in the role. Ability to undertake this type of a pre-employment decision will very much depend on the experience of the professional and having possession of a good vocational assessment report. Establishing the effects of cognitive impairment on workplace activity will enable the introduction of appropriate strategies to overcome potential difficulties. However, the often subtle nature of brain injury will mean that it is not always feasible to identify the likely problems without trial and error on the job itself. This will entail the client working under close supervision, so that identification of difficult aspects of a job can be made. Identification can be achieved by detailing oversights/omissions/detours in the client's workplace performance, enabling patterns of difficulty to be established and appropriate action to deal with problems implemented.

Vocational assessment

A valuable piece of information which can be used in conjunction with a specialist cognitive report is a vocational (work) assessment. Vocational assessment is an ongoing process insomuch as the goals and ambitions broaden as recovery is achieved. An ongoing vocational assessment will identify the subtle cognitive issues that come to light as more complex activity is undertaken in a work role. A vocational assessment can usually be carried out by a disability employment officer, vocational assessor, careers guidance, occupational psychologist, employment adviser or occupational therapist.

As the name implies, a vocational assessment is a review of an individual's work capabilities. The issues assessed on a vocational assessment can be varied and are very much dependent upon the client's vocational aspirations. It can cover aptitudes, workplace competencies, personality, literacy, numeric skill, IT skills, occupational interest as well as a number of other relevant areas. Vocational assessment is only really suited to those individuals with mild to moderate cognitive impairment. Individuals with severe brain injury are unlikely to be work ready and the results from vocational assessment will quickly become obsolete as the client recovers.

The primary purpose of vocational assessment is to help an individual with a disability choose appropriate employment. This may be a return to their former job, a relocation to new duties with their present work position or a completely new type of job. It will help identify strengths and weaknesses as well as identifying transferable skills, areas of rehabilitation need and shortfalls in personal interactive skill which can be developed. The outcome should be to provide an individual with greater awareness of themselves, enabling them to make an informed career choice.

The vocational assessor's role is to establish workplace competence, and they should consequently consider the impact of poor cognitive functioning on work performance, as well as on the assessment process itself. It is essential to ensure that skills being assessed are not unduly affected by cognitive deficit. For example, a client assessed on their verbal reasoning ability, who fails to concentrate because of attentional problems, will inevitably receive an overall low score. However, poor attention is not the same as poor verbal reasoning ability. The client may otherwise have intact verbal skill, but momentarily cannot access this due to inability to concentrate long enough to undertake a timed task. In this instance, ensure you assess the verbal skill and not their ability to concentrate. Similarly, poor short-term verbal memory will have an impact on the individual's ability to retain the instructions of a task. Consequently their poor performance may well be due to inability to remember instructions and not necessarily poor ability to undertake the task at hand. Poor motor skills, poor speech, depression, poor vision or being in a degree of pain will all adversely affect the client's ability to either answer the assessor's questions or complete an answer sheet.

Clients with any acquired disability, but particularly a brain injury, invariably have low stamina and tire easily. There is a cumulative effect, so that regardless of providing ample breaks throughout the assessment period (or in their job), as the day proceeds, the client becomes progressively tired and they have a decreasing ability to sustain concentration. They can leave an assessment exhausted in the evening, but may not sleep because there is so much new information to be processed and assimilated in the brain's structures. The next day they come to the assessment process, not having been refreshed by sleep. More positive outcomes can be gained if the assessment process is over a longer time period, perhaps one or two hours per day or whatever is appropriate for the client's actual ability to sustain the rigorous demands of an assessment.

Assessing basic skills

Basic skills are the ability to read and write and in general to communicate. It also involves an ability to use numeric skill to function adequately in work and in society. These are viewed as essential skills for success in employment and in everyday living. More recently Information Technology (IT skill) is considered a basic requirement for employment success. Basic skills are the building blocks of the educational curriculum.

An individual's reading and writing ability has obvious importance in gaining and sustaining employment in today's job market. It is also a skill often damaged by brain injury. Consequently it is one of the main work competences for a vocational assessor to consider evaluating. Establishing the client's ability to deal with written language provides at least some indication of how successful they are likely to be in this part of the job.

Written communication (for employment purposes) can be described as the ability to produce written text (write) and the ability to read competently. As a basic, you need to ensure that the client is capable of reading and understanding essential industrial safety notices such as *Fire Exit* and *Dangerous Machinery* if these warnings are likely to apply to their work environment. There are a number of instruments available that assess written communication skill in more depth, which are available from suppliers of test material.[2] The appropriate assessment material can be chosen in relation to whatever level you wish to assess at.

Access to assessment materials is usually restricted to individuals trained to understand and interpret the material.

To enable the assessor to formally assess at an approximately relevant level, they will be required to make some sort of informal judgement of the client's written communication skills. If the written communication tasks (or assessment tasks in general) are too easy, it may feel condescending. Too difficult and it will be demotivating. The complexity level of assessment tasks should also correlate to the complexity of the job and the vocational aspirations of the client concerned. Pre-accident written communication skills and intellectual functioning can be estimated by previous jobs held or by educational qualifications.

As with verbal skills, inability to count or poor counting skill can make it difficult to sustain work. The most mundane low-skilled task can require the client to count widgets into a box. Numerical deficit as a consequence of brain injury can include disorders of calculation such as the inability to understand the borrow/carry rule in subtraction or the understanding and processing of arithmetic symbols. Assessment of numerical capability is relatively straightforward. It can be achieved by giving the client numeric sums assessing basic operations of the four rules of number. Calculations should be assessed using both paper and pencil and undertaking calculations in their head. When undertaking calculations, it is quite feasible that adults forget basic operational rules in calculations and it is often true that some never learned them in the first place. You need to use your judgement and available information to deduce if inability to undertake a task is a cognitive issue or a knowledge issue.

If the individual is aspiring to return to work with numbers/figures as a career, possibly as clerical officer or in accounting of some description, you may need to test their skill further by using one of the many numerical reasoning tasks available from providers of assessment material. With severe cognitive problems, you may be required to assess more basic ability such as their ability to identify coinage and undertake the purchasing of items of small value.

The other major area considered as a basic skill is Information Technology. It was not until relatively recently that IT skills formed part of the National Curriculum, consequently the older client may not have any experience in computing. For those clients with experience of IT, a review of retained IT skill can easily be achieved by a systematic assessment of basic word processing skill. As with other areas of basic skill, there is no reason to establish competence beyond what they are likely to apply in the workplace.

If the client is unable to undertake basic calculations or has problems with written communication, or poor IT skills likely to impact on their job performance, then training in these areas should form part of their overall vocational rehabilitation programme or work development training, regardless of whether the problem is cognitive in origin or due to the fact that they have received poor tutoring in these areas.

Assessing higher level cognitive skill

As with cognitive assessment, the formal tools of vocational assessment can be extremely limited in establishing the workplace competence of a brain-injured employee. Psychometric tests do not always simulate typical work environments. One problem with most formal psychometric tests is that they do not provide much more than a percentile score, which is not particularly productive when planning a development and rehabilitation programme or a return to work programme. Formal assessment tools also measure the skill in isolation, when skills of the workplace are a combination of attributes and the dynamics between attributes. To obtain a more holistic understanding of workplace ability, it is necessary to look beyond standardized assessment and this can be achieved by competency exercises. There are many off-the-shelf competency assessment tools. When working with brain injury, it is best to spend a little time and develop specific assessment tools, which should be bespoke in line with the needs of the client. This is not a difficult task to undertake.

A workplace competency is a skill or knowledge that we have which enables us to carry out our work successfully. It is not a taught skill in the mould of basic skills described above, such as numeracy, literacy or IT, nor is it a learned vocational skill, such as mechanics, joinery or cooking. Competencies are skills we acquire over a lifetime, through our interaction with others and at a subconscious level. Some examples of work competencies are leadership, interpersonal sensitivity, liaising and negotiation or team working. This type of skill can be broadly grouped as executive skills. A competency exercise is an assessment task which has been specifically researched and designed to capture a person's ability to undertake this type of workplace activity. It is about assessing observable behaviours, how an individual has acted and why they have taken the particular decisions that they have. Competencies are usually assessed in a group setting so that interactive skills and the more subtle team dynamics can be assessed. Individuals are assessed on a range of competencies. The term Assessment Centre is usually applied to this multi-factorial approach. Competency assessment has its origin in the field of human resources and in occupational psychology.

Historically, competency assessment (Assessment Centres) is undertaken to assess a candidate's suitability for employment (job selection), at middle management level and above. It can nevertheless act as an excellent tool to be adapted to assess a brain-injured person's workplace competence. Abilities measured in this process will be related to identified deficits or with competencies needed to carry out the client's job successfully. When undertaking the assessment of brain-injured clients, their performance should be reviewed by a number of knowledgeable and experienced staff, who arrive at a consensus about the participant's capabilities in a particular area. With a number of assessors involved, there is more opportunity to pick up the subtle, sometimes unnoticeable cognitive problems, and bring them forward for discussion. Areas where difficulties have emerged can be considered areas for further rehabilitation and development. Performance is rated in relation to that expected of the type of job they aspire returning to. Their performance should not be measured against the abilities of the other participants involved in the process.

Competency assessment is ideal for a vocational rehabilitation setting where there are a number of clients going through the vocational assessment process. With appropriate planning and sufficient staff, it would be feasible to assess different clients on different competencies within this group setting. The information gained from such assessments should always be fed back to the client for discussion and to ascertain why he or she acted in a particular way. With the client's permission, you can videotape the work which enables the client to review the situation from a neutral perspective, providing some insight into behaviour and performance. Competency exercises can also be designed to act as rehabilitation tools, for the development of skills that are essential for job retention, but where the client has performed poorly.

Example competency exercises

- *In-tray exercise:* The client is asked to review an office in-tray of reports, letters, messages, memoranda etc. The client is provided with criteria and asked to prioritize, organize and generally deal with the information. You can discuss performance with pre-agreed performance standards as well as the reasoning behind their decisions and actions. This can be undertaken in the workplace, mimicking closely their actual job duties but without the dangers of costly mistakes.

- *Meeting the client:* In this exercise the client meets an external customer to discuss issues relevant to the job. In a rehabilitation environment, the customer role can be played by a member of staff or another willing client. If this is undertaken in the actual workplace, the external customer would be substituted with role play in sensitive work, where the employer would fear losing business with a real purchaser.

Exploring alternative employment (career guidance)

Typically the cognitive problems incurred by a brain-injured individual are such that they will be required to accept a less demanding occupational role. Problems with memory, concentration and executive problems limit the individual choices in terms of future career. The type of work that they will be capable of will correlate with recovery in these areas. The vocational assessor will at some stage need to review what employment options are available to their client. This review may not be necessary on the first occasion you meet, but as and when the person's capabilities are established, there is a need to explore what employment is likely to be available. In the final event, when exploring potential career paths, you need to work to the particular strengths of the person, which may be their voice, physical capabilities or interpersonal skills.

You can expect that any revision of career downwards will be met with some resentment and anger from the individual concerned. This is entirely natural and part of the recovery process. For many of us, our social life revolves around our job, our friends are work colleagues and often we describe ourselves by what job we do. For the more skilled employee, there will have been many years dedicated to developing a skill base. A less demanding job usually implies a less prestigious role, reduced remuneration and a loss of self-esteem. It is hardly surprising that some individuals will feel resentful at the loss of a career. However, most are accepting over the longer term.

Assessing occupational interest is best viewed as a process of elimination rather than identification, eliminating jobs in which the individual has no interest or does not have the cognitive capabilities to succeed. This reduces the amount of information to work with and allows focus on the types of work, where the person has every prospect of succeeding. Pressure from the client, family members and other rehabilitation professionals can lead to the inexperienced vocational assessor feeling a sense of failure, if they have not identified the 'ideal job' for their brain-injured client. It is perfectly reasonable, in my view, that a brain-injured client concludes a job interest search without knowing exactly what career they would like, but with a much narrower range to consider. This is entirely acceptable considering that cognitive function may improve, further increasing the complexity of work they could aspire to. Realistic expectations of outcomes likely to be achieved should be discussed at the outset, to ensure that both the client and the employment professional do not feel they have failed.

In terms of choice of job, people generally fall into two categories. First are those who look upon employment simply for financial gain, to pay their mortgage and bills, and take care of their family. The second group are career-focused. Over and above financial remuneration, they crave fulfilment and personal development. A problem that exists with the second group (often professionals and managers) is that when they re-evaluate their work interest, it is difficult for them to revise down. They have a tendency to consider other professions or managerial positions.

By and large one specialized field is as complex as another and problems encountered in one professional setting are likely to manifest in other similar work environments. All that will be achieved by exploring other jobs at similar levels enjoyed prior to the injury will be the added burden and cost of having to retrain. If indications are that the person is not able to undertake their existing professional or managerial role, they need to be guided to revise down, with the proviso that if they demonstrate themselves to be capable of working at the reduced level, there is nothing preventing them trying to work their way up to a similar job enjoyed prior to the sustained injury.

In reviewing potential areas of employment, focus the client on the requirements of each position in relation to qualifications needed, practicality of obtaining employment, remuneration, skills needed to perform the work, personal employment interests and personal capabilities. Invite them to note down the advantages and disadvantages of each job they have expressed an interest in, with the above mentioned requirements to be taken into consideration in the process. Impractical job choices, including those likely to be affected by cognitive problems, can, after discussion and agreement from the client, be eliminated. Rank ordering the remaining jobs in terms of preference should help to provide some sort of career focus. Job ranking can be undertaken in terms of high-medium-low preference or first choice, second choice or third choice.

Clients with severe injury can express great hope for a complete change of career field, often with the view of securing employment in computing. The reason behind this is that while physically they are limited, they can access computers. Information Technology as a field for employment has in my experience exaggerated the opportunities that are available. While some clients will successfully carve out new careers in Information Technology, it is easy to underestimate just how competitive this field is and how difficult it could be to gain paid employment.

Personality

Personality testing is widely used in industry for assessment and selection at graduate and managerial level. An assessment of an individual's personality allows the identification of interpersonal skills, often required for successful employment where interaction or negotiation is a requirement. Personality testing was initially used for personal development in managers. Increasingly, it is used for personal development for individuals who have a disability. Used appropriately, it can help to rebuild confidence, give a sense of self and identify areas for further development.

Personality testing can be extremely rewarding for a brain-injured client who struggles to make sense of who they are and what they are doing following the acquisition of a life-changing disability. If you do decide to use such an assessment measure, it must be very restricted. It is definitely not to be used with clients with severe cognitive problems, probably not with clients with a moderate cognitive injury and with a great deal of caution with clients with a mild brain injury. The assessor should take all relevant information into consideration before using such an instrument. This includes deciding if the client has stabilized, do they have insight into themselves and are they sufficiently reflective. Do they understand the language and the concepts involved in the personality questionnaire? These principles apply to any self-completion questionnaire. You may also consider asking a close relative or friend to comment on any changes in personality they have noticed.

A common question that is asked when a client with an acquired brain injury is confronted with completing a self-rating questionnaire such as a personality test is should they answer as they are now, how they were prior to the accident or how they would like to be in the future. While this is a valid question for anybody using such an instrument, it has obvious relevance to an individual whose life has been dramatically and irreversibly changed. The only response to this question can be to answer any self-rating questionnaire as the person they are now. This is the only certainty that they have. If they have had a personality test undertaken prior to the accident (which is unusual) then a comparison can be helpful to gauge change. With research, perhaps personality tests can be adapted and used more to determine the nature of change of personality caused by cognitive injury.

Risk assessment

Health and safety is the 'Catch 22' situation of returning a brain-injured individual to employment. On one hand, they need the work-related experience to improve while on the other, safety can be jeopardized if the individual is not fully capable of undertaking the role. The law imposes a responsibility on employers to ensure safety in the workplace for all employees. Failure to do so can lead to an employer being sued for personal injury. It can be a struggle to persuade an employer of the minimal risk involved in accepting your client back into the workplace. You can have some appreciation if not sympathy with the employer's perspective. An employer nevertheless should take all reasonable steps to reduce risk and assess the risk against the cost of eliminating any risk involved.

A systematic risk assessment should be undertaken to determine the client's capabilities and potential dangers to the client and to others. There is a five-step guide to risk analysis. The Health and Safety Executive can be approached for guidance on this issue. Special consideration needs to be given when considering the health and safety implications of individuals with cognitive problems.

1. *Recognize the dangers:* where there is a threat of an accident to the client or another employee. For example, floors that are lined or checked can cause particular difficulty with vision and proprioception leaving the client with poor balance.

2. *Identify who is at risk:* Broaden the assessment to a wider range than the client. Identify how others might be injured or how loss might affect the company employing them.

3. *Evaluate the special circumstance:* Are existing precautions sufficient or are more complex safety measures required?

4. *Record findings:* You are not the only person working with this person. This information needs to be shared. The

client's confidentiality should not be compromised so sharing information should be on a need-to-know basis.

5. *Review:* Review risks in line with the client's changing abilities.

Other modes of information gathering

Information regarding the client's capabilities and interpersonal skills can also be gained from the referring agent; through informal observation of the behaviour and actions of the person; and through responses to questions by family members or by the client themselves. It is useful to co-ordinate resources with other professionals involved with clients: welfare, social services, occupational health department, so that there is a bank of information.

A degree of caution should be applied when preparing and providing reports following vocational assessment. There is a growing trend towards making all information available to clients. Consequently it is important that they are constructed in a manner that the client can comprehend: both in terms of the language and the concepts involved. Professionals and employers involved in helping the client return to employment are unlikely to have the time to read in-depth reports. A one-page summary of required action should be produced, which will have every prospect of being read by others working with your client.

Final thoughts

The assessment of brain-injured clients is not a straightforward process. You are assessing a person who only a few weeks or months ago held a responsible job and in all probability was happy and comfortable with their place in society, a place that took decades of hard slog to achieve. Acquiring a brain injury could bring a complete reversal where before the injury they managed others, but now feel they are the ones under supervision. Everything has been taken from them, including their independence. They have the additional worry of how they are to provide for their family.

For the above mentioned reason, some assessment tasks just do not work for this group and there can be a negative reaction. With any assessment task, be it ability or occupational interest, or personality assessment, if it is not being undertaken successfully or there is a negative reaction to it, for whatever reason, do not be afraid to halt the assessment and try something else. However, it is important that you do not convey the impression to the client that in some way they have failed.

Notes

1 'Neurological assessment' is sometimes used interchangeably with 'cognitive assessment'. Strictly speaking the neurologist is the only person to undertake a neurological exam.

2 Assessment tools are available from suppliers such the Psychological Corporation and NFER Nelson. There is stringent control on access to material to ensure that the user is properly trained in their use. Information on appropriate training and providers of quality assessment material can be obtained from the British Psychological Society.

Chapter 6

Vocational Rehabilitation

There are few events more traumatic and life changing than acquiring a brain injury as an adult. It is tragic for the older, retired person but it is has far greater implications for a working-aged man or woman, with a family to support but unable to retain a job to provide them with an income. In these circumstances, it can be absolutely devastating. Regardless of how bleak the future looks, with appropriate support people can and do return to employment.

The nature and complexity of brain injury is such that good recovery is dependent upon a holistic and skilful intervention from a multidisciplinary team. This enables the broad and varied needs of the individual to be catered for. Currently there are two main approaches to rehabilitation, both multidisciplinary in nature. I suspect in the future there will be an amalgamation of the two approaches, creating a smooth path of progression for the client's development.

The first of these approaches is the medical approach to rehabilitation, which stems from the health service where rehabilitation is medical intervention, therapeutic, hospital-based and aimed at initial survival of injury and minimizing of disability. Rehabilitation is viewed in terms of acute health care. This type of intervention is generally shorter-based.

The second approach, which is outlined in this chapter, is the post-acute (vocational) or social approach, which is practical and trial and error-based, aimed at reintegrating the client into the complexities of the workplace and the social requirements of the community. Vocational rehabilitation can be extremely effective in helping return people to work following a traumatic brain injury (Turner-Stokes 1999). Early referral to vocational rehabilitation is tantamount to positive outcomes and will significantly improve work potential.

Vocational rehabilitation is a collection of therapeutic supports which are co-ordinated and combined with practical work experience. There are a number of broad aims of vocational rehabilitation but it is best described as preparing the client to enter or retrain for employment. It acts as a supportive stepping stone from disability into the world of work. It is intended to help the individual recover as much functional ability as they can, minimizing the impact of the injuries on the rest of their lives, particularly in relation to work. Vocational rehabilitation is a fairly long-term requirement of about six months' duration. Individuals with acquired brain injury are continually improving and developing, consequently there is no clear entry point or exit point, but a continuous process which can last into the workplace and beyond. Although brain-injured individuals have special needs, vocational rehabilitation units generally provide services to people returning to the labour market with all types of disability. Some units nevertheless will specialize in brain injury.

Severely brain-injured clients require experienced in-depth professional intervention, specialist skills and specialized facilities. Consequently this group are unlikely to be in the position of seeking employment until further improvement has been attained. They are likely to benefit from a supportive medical model of rehabilitation. Vocational rehabilitation is generally populated with moderately impaired clients who are able to concentrate on goals and have a degree of functional independence. A key criteria for consideration before vocational rehabilitation is a viable option is that the person's condition is stable and not likely to deteriorate.

Clients with moderate brain injury nonetheless still require access to a wide range of therapeutic support. Professional staff will work on a raft of measures aimed at increasing their overall skill base. This may include dealing with the residual emotional difficulties such as anger and resentment associated with the loss of abilities and changing lifestyle. Therapeutic intervention will also focus on increasing functional capacity, relearning routine tasks, introducing self-management programmes, and focus on maximizing independence. Staff will support clients on developing existing skills, acquiring new skills, exploring vocational opportunities, developing interpersonal skills, acclimatizing to new environments and will provide appropriate work experience which enables the client to rebuild their confidence and self-belief. Rehabilitation consequently requires enormous input and mental effort from the client.

Properly constructed vocational rehabilitation should endeavour to provide graded exposure to increasingly complex work tasks, at a pace that enables the client to maximize their occupational potential. Part of this therapeutic strategy will be aimed at helping the individual gain some insight into any difficulties that they are experiencing, while providing support needed to adapt and come to terms with their reduced capabilities. Underpinning this is neuropsychological assistance which will help increase motivation and perseverance in the face of difficult life changes.

It can be easy for clients to become pessimistic about their future, which can hinder rehabilitation. Pessimism can be a natural part of the trials and tribulations of the improvement and recovery process. Throughout rehabilitation, clients should be encouraged by positive reinforcement to put such thoughts into perspective, counteracting negative thoughts with a positive argument, to add some balance to the various concerns which can, if not discussed openly with the client, be overwhelming. Nevertheless, it is also vital to relay to the client what realistic improvements are likely, so that they do not assume unfair expectations.

Issues to consider when providing a vocational rehabilitation programme

Holistic approach

Vocational rehabilitation must be holistic in nature. To be successful it should address all the issues and barriers to employment as well as the dynamics and interplay between the cognitive, emotional and psychological issues. It should include a degree of individualistic therapeutic interventions including counselling, occupational therapy and cognitive rehabilitation therapy. It also needs to contain a degree of group work. Group work such as social therapy provides the client with an opportunity to share experiences with people who have travelled a similar journey. Often it is the best way of enabling them to come to terms with the changes.

Inclusion

Vocational rehabilitation is ideally a two-way process in which the client 'buys into' the benefits of such a programme. The programme manager should ensure that the client does not feel left in the dark about the way forward for them.

Case conferences

A case conference is a review to discuss with the client their progress and changes to their rehabilitation programme or workplacement. The inclusion of regular case conferences can help to ensure that appropriate progress is achieved and that support for the client is adequate. Case conferences should not be top heavy with professional staff, which can be intimidating for the individual concerned. Preferably they should be one to one with either the case manager or key worker. Family members often like to be included and this on the whole is to be welcomed, providing the feedback is aimed at the client and not over their head.

Timetable

Clients should be provided with a framework from which they can gauge progress. They also need to understand why they are undertaking particular activities. Explain the longer-term structure of the programme and how the course aims to support and develop them, and how it will help them reintegrate back into employment. Provide an overall plan of activity (personal timetable), covering the whole of the rehabilitation course. This will afford some indication of expected progress over a longer timescale. The client's personal timetable would include the dates for case conferences and could also be a convenient place to record the goals to be achieved/assessments to be made before each conference.

Goal setting

Rehabilitation goals will be different for each individual. Include the client in setting their own goals. Explain to the client in what way the goals agreed will be achieved and why the therapeutic modules they will undertake have been recommended. Ensure that the individual's personal goals are the same as the goals the rehabilitation team have planned. Provide timescales where possible so that progress can be measured. Long-term plans/goals will almost certainly need to be reviewed, depending on the progression and development of the individual involved.

Regular reviews

An increase in functional capability can bring with it negative as well as positive feelings, which the rehabilitation staff should be sensitive to. Regular reviews are therefore essential as brain-injured clients' requirements will change as they progress and develop through vocational rehabilitation, often in unpredictable ways. Continual and ongoing revision of the individual's progress will identify changes in capabilities and emotions as well as introduce new therapeutic interventions. For example, increasing awareness (insight) of cognitive problems brings with it the realization of significant and lifelong disability, which could possibly lead to the client becoming depressed. Reviews should also be about identifying therapeutic interventions that are not working and should no longer be implemented, as well as identifying which therapeutic interventions have been successful but are no longer necessary.

Clients can have ongoing issues not directly related to their rehabilitation. Problems can be financial or social in nature or due to being in an unfamiliar environment, often away from supportive family and friends. Regular liaison with a key worker enables support to be provided in all the issues related to the potential barriers to the client's development and well-being.

Including family

Inclusion of the family where possible is always advisable at the rehabilitation stage in the client's recovery. Family members are the people who bring continuity to the life-changing experience and the journey that the brain-injured client has travelled. They will support the client long after formal vocational rehabilitation has ceased. Family and friends have a valuable source of knowledge that the rehabilitation team need to tap into, such as past educational achievements, employment or personality changes that the client themselves may not be aware of. They also provide valuable support at a crucial stage in the client's progression. The rehabilitation team would benefit from looking at ways in which they can include the family, building relationships with them. The family could also be provided with a timetable of activity, be invited to case conferences if the client agrees and offered regular accurate updates.

Plain language

Adopt a plain English approach to the language used within a vocational rehabilitation setting and in the reports which are produced for client or professional consumption. Avoid the temptation to add pseudo-credibility to the programme by the adoption of ostentatious words which have clinical connotations. Consider the client's perspective. For example, *prior to injury* is more palatable than *premorbid*, and *below average* sounds better than *mentally substandard*. Use common sense in the employment of language used to discuss therapeutic interventions.

Work placement

A large part of vocational rehabilitation is support into a practical workplacement, preferably with an external commercial organization or ideally with the client's current employer. Returning the brain-injured client to the workplace as soon as possible is one of the cornerstones to success. A quick return to work also ensures that work becomes the norm rather than some therapeutic establishment. Gaining an appropriate workplace is not easy, particularly if it is not with the existing employer. However, employers are usually more enthusiastic if external support to the client is provided.

The brain-injured person will possibly continue to improve and develop. The initial vocational placement will need to be reviewed and this should be scheduled in as part of the requirement. It should be seen as a dynamic situation rather than a fixed one. The presentation of it in this way to the client also helps them accept the lower-level employment initially offered to them. Clients need to have hope and the opportunity to express the natural human tendency to transcend and to explore.

In placing the client in an appropriate workplacement, the employer is entitled to be informed of issues that are going to impact in an environment for which they have a responsibility. It is important to discuss with the client and obtain approval for the level of disclosure of which you feel the employer needs to be aware. Identify the positive contribution your client can provide to the employer but be realistic and agree what support you can provide. There is little advantage in underplaying any difficulties the client has in order to secure a placement. You will only disappoint a potential source of work experience once, probably never getting the opportunity to do so again for another client. Think long term and of building networks and relationships.

Vocational therapeutic techniques

A number of techniques have developed over the years through psychology and counselling and from other disciplines, which is used to improve cognitive functioning. As with most fields of science, there is a great deal of debate as to the effectiveness of these interventions. Readers need to form their own judgements as to the effectiveness of a particular therapeutic intervention.

Cognitive rehabilitation

Most cognitive recovery is attained in the first six months. However, there will be further opportunity for recovery both spontaneously without intervention and through cognitive rehabilitation. After the first year or two, progress/improvement is slow and not always apparent, but it can be achieved. There can be significant leaps of progress after quite extended periods of time. Cognitive rehabilitation provides an opportunity for brain-injured clients to practise functions of the brain that have been damaged through injury. It supports the brain's natural ability to impose order and pattern from the information that the client has in front of them. This may include such cognitive skills as visual processing, decision making, memory and concentration. In some ways it is similar to physiotherapy exercises, developing a client's physical ability following a muscular skeletal injury. While cognition and physical capability are different entities, both share the principle that without practice, there is unlikely to be improvement. Cognitive rehabilitation therefore refers to intervention to help practise cognitive factors in the hope that this will improve function.

Cognitive rehabilitation operates on the foundation that only practice will improve performance and increase confidence in using the skill. A second foundation for cognitive rehabilitation comes from the view that other parts of the brain can be encouraged to take over existing cognitive functions when damage to a part of the brain has occurred. This rewiring process is only likely to occur on the initial stages of brain injury (first two years), consequently the earlier the intervention the better.

Cognitive methods

In the unlikely event that you find yourself, as a vocational expert, working with severely brain-injured clients, suitable computer games can act as good cognitive rehabilitation tools and are excellent for hand-eye co-ordination, visual processing, concentration and memory. The visual interaction and easy success can also capture the person's interest and act to boost confidence. As the client improves, they can progress to jigsaw puzzles, which promote improvements in spatial awareness, hand-eye co-ordination, concentration and logical analysis. More sophisticated cognitive rehabilitation methods are available for clients who have progressed from the acute stage. This includes *Brainwave-R* (Malia *et al.* 1997) which provides a practical opportunity to develop deficit areas, focusing on functional areas across a wide range of skills.[1] *Brainwave-R* contains a wide range of individualistic therapies that can be used to increase performance.

Cognitive rehabilitation should be undertaken in conjunction with aids and adaptations such as memory prompts which may provide additional support. External strategies including a diary for planning appointments, wall calendar, electronic memory aids, mobile phones, writing down lists of things to do, notes and post-its, watches and alarms are all everyday devices that can be adopted for assisting memory. A checklist can be used to ensure a necessary sequence of steps is followed in order to complete a task. These types of aids and adaptations are useful at the acute phase of rehabilitation, although having served their original function they can become more of a problem than a solution. Part of the vocational rehabilitation process should entail identifying adaptations and strategies that are no longer useful but more likely to hinder than help recovery.

As well as giving the individual an opportunity to practise essential cognitive skills, cognitive rehabilitation is, in my experience, as much about working through emotional factors such as confidence, anxiety and embarrassment which prohibit the individual from giving it 100 per cent. Clients are often reluctant to try tasks simply because they know they are not going to be good at them. They become embarrassed at their poor performance on a task, a task which they view as fairly basic and automatic. It can also serve to reinforce the extent of their disability. Cognitive rehabilitation enables them to practise a skill in a safe environment and at a level that is comfortable for them. Cognitive problems should not be addressed in isolation but simultaneously with the emotional issues that occur, due to both the damage itself and the traumatic change of lifestyle forced upon the individual.

Work-related cognitive rehabilitation

The ultimate aim for most brain-injured clients is to return to employment, preferably to their previous job. Hopefully they will be as work ready as possible when returning to the actual workplace but there are always going to be tasks that are difficult for them. It is this transition from a vocational rehabilitation unit into workplace rehabilitation that workplace cognitive rehabilitation therapy should aim to facilitate. Cognitive rehabilitation for the workplace should be bespoke, designed for the different needs of each individual. You can maximize effectiveness by taking steps to identify the patterns and consistencies within work duties that the client has difficulty with. There is little in the way of commercially available training for cognitive rehabilitation methods in relation to the workplace because it is so individualistic but common sense is the most valuable asset. It is often a matter of identifying the work-related problem through observation or appropriate assessment of capabilities and having detailed knowledge of job requirements. Methods of identifying this information are discussed in various sections throughout the book.

Cognitive rehabilitation in the workplace should be active rather than passive. People are more likely to retain information if they have been involved in the decision-making process. For example, a motorist who takes the decisions when driving is more likely to remember the way to a particular location on the next trip than the passenger who has been sitting with passive interest. Cognitive rehabilitation tasks should mimic job duties as closely as possible. Break job duties down into achievable goals from which cognitive rehabilitation tasks can be created. Set increasingly difficult tasks to work towards. Build on small successes, as failures tend to reinforce poor self-esteem. Record progress and make positive contrasts between present and past performance. Give feedback accurately to clients in terms and concepts they can relate to.

Most clients feel they should be starting on more complex cognitive rehabilitation tasks than they are actually capable of. Previously high- functioning individuals can be the most reluctant to undertake cognitive rehabilitation tasks which they view as basic or beneath their capabilities. When delivering work-related cognitive rehabilitation, operate on the basis that the client will need to build levels of capability as stepping stones to returning to working at their full potential. Work towards building a new work life, rather than restoring the old.

While support can be gained from cognitive rehabilitation specialists, employment professionals should take the main lead in devising and selecting appropriate therapeutic interventions, which should mimic as realistically as possible the tasks that the client has difficulty with. This is akin to creating work competency exercises. Cognitive rehabilitation tasks should simulate real-life work tasks but without mistakes having a negative impact for the employer.

Principles of cognitive rehabilitation in the workplace

- The brain is not hard wired but can rewire so that other non-damaged parts of the brain can take over responsibilities.

- Cognitive rehabilitation should be bespoke to the individual's needs where possible.

- The programme should be aimed as far as possible at the client's level of ability. Too little and they will stagnate; too much and it can have an adverse effect on confidence.

- By undertaking simulations of a task, improvements can be made on this task. Consequently work-related cognitive rehabilitation should simulate workplace tasks as closely as possible.

- Cognitive rehabilitation therapy should be undertaken as soon as possible after the injury and should continue for as long as is necessary. This will likely occur over a protracted period (sometimes a lifetime). Adjustment should be made according to the client's changing needs.

- Improving performance on one cognitive factor is likely to have a positive effect on other cognitive factors.

- Increasing awareness and accepting that some tasks are beyond their present capabilities are parts of the remit of cognitive rehabilitation.

- Health and safety is the principal concern in workplace rehabilitation.

Literacy

There are many occupation-related skills essential to employment but common to brain injury, which may need to be addressed within the vocational rehabilitation setting, if the client is to return to some form of employment. In particular are the skills of communication which 'oil the wheels' of participation in work-related activity. Written communication skill is vital to employability and promotion in the workplace.

Acquired literacy problems vary from minor impairment such as reduced spelling ability, to having lost all ability to read or write. Textual information effectively becomes a foreign language. The client's literacy skills should be evaluated at the assessment stage.

The starting point for the rehabilitation of clients who have severe literacy problems will be reviewing letters of the alphabet, with a view to establishing what letters they recognize. Rehabilitation should include the provision of literacy training to rebuild their skills. For clients with moderate impairment, written communication can be improved by such work tasks as basic copy exercises and computer data entry exercises, slowly building up writing/reading skills from words to basic sentences and where possible progressing to paragraphs. If at some stage the client aspires to return to education, they may need to relearn the form and conventions of essay and letter writing.

Speech

Speech rehabilitation, in my view and experience, is different than input from speech therapists. Speech rehabilitation concentrates on psychological factors such as confidence and anxiety. The speech therapist can help the client in relearning basic muscle movements and sounds.

Speech production, where it has been impaired through brain injury, can be enhanced by exposure and practice in formulating words and sentences. This can include specifically created group work engaging the client in conversations. This type of exercise will have the added bonus of informally exercising verbal memory. Within a vocational rehabilitational setting, structured group work and video feedback to clients can provide awareness of the nature of speech problems, providing the client with a greater awareness of the speech impediment they are experiencing. Client consent would be required before proceeding with this. Another speech rehabilitation exercise that can be useful is free word association, which can help the speed of processing of verbal information. This involves the vocational professional saying a word (any word) and the client as quickly as they can recount the first word that comes to mind without censoring their thoughts.

Unlike Freudian counselling, there is no attempt made to analyse the response.

Speech recovery is impeded when the individual concerned becomes self-conscious and frustrated with their difficulty at articulation, resulting in their withdrawal from communication. Without practice, speech improvements cannot be achieved. The speech rehabilitation programme CRISP (Cognitive Rehabilitation Individual Speech Programme) aims to provide a safe, non-threatening opportunity to improve speech at an early stage following injury.

Dexterity

An area for particular attention on a work-related vocational rehabilitation programme is dexterity. Where one arm/hand is weaker than the other, activity should be encouraged to strengthen the weaker hand. This can be achieved through therapeutic exercise or by deliberate use of the weaker hand for tasks. Similarly, where the client needs to be able to use both hands simultaneously, tasks can be selected for this purpose. Learning to touch type, for example, can act as a valuable therapeutic measure in terms of increasing bilateral dexterity and can provide the client with a valuable work skill, making them more employable.

Behavioural management

Many employers or inexperienced staff will have particular difficulty with unpredictability or aggressiveness which can form part of the underlying problems facing the brain-injured group. This reaction is normal and characteristic of lack of experience. In a work environment, behavioural management techniques can be applied. Behavioural management intervention requires universal and consistent responses to behaviour by management/colleagues or staff, if it is to be effective. Reinforcement of behavioural management techniques in terms of praise and encouragement has been known to be beneficial.

Counselling

Clients need an opportunity to talk about their loss, including loss of personal autonomy, loss of function, loss of confidence, loss of dreams, loss of ambition but above all a loss of sense of self. Client-centered counselling is useful in helping the client adjust to their new lifestyle. It can help support the move from the survival stage to the adaptive functional stage. They will need support and encouragement in creating and following through on their own initiatives. They will also need support in conquering their many fears, both rational and irrational, which prevent them from maximizing their potential.

Cognitive behavioural therapy (CBT)[2] can also be a pretty effective therapeutic intervention. The basis of CBT is the challenging of a negative belief system, discussing and reviewing the beliefs held, beliefs which often derive from adverse experiences.

From vocational rehabilitation to the workplace

The transfer from a rehabilitation environment to the workplace can be a difficult one. Vocational rehabilitation units are by their nature safe and secure places for the client. They provide contact with a group who share similar experiences and they provide stimulation and daily activity. Despite a client being frustrated at the slow progress they feel they are making, when the day dawns for them to start a work placement or return to their job, there can occasionally be a reluctance to move from the safety and familiarity of the vocational rehabilitation unit.

It may be necessary in the short term to delay the workplacement, but it is important that the true issues causing the reluctance are identified and dealt with. Assurance can be given that support is not being withdrawn but a new phase of the development is being entered. It is essential that this is how the client views it.

Clients need time to make the psychological adjustment to their disability and the accompanying reductions of their skills. The general rehabilitation strategy to help someone return to work following brain injury is to ease them back in gently, usually on a part-time basis with a mentor and other support mechanisms and with monitoring on a regular basis. Initially provide tasks where the requirements of the job are self-evident. This approach enables you to ascertain the consequences of neurological deficit on work ability, as well as identifying adaptations or training that can be introduced to facilitate and support further recovery.

When returning the client to the actual workplace, do not overstretch them or you may well cause a setback. Retraining needs to be regulated in accordance with the abilities and stamina of the client to apply themselves to the training. An unfamiliar situation or training event can be more exhausting than a normal day's work activity, due to the demands placed on concentration and memory when learning new material.

Final thoughts

This chapter has focused on vocational rehabilitation in terms of therapeutic intervention. Most people return to employment without this type of support but would nevertheless benefit from vocational rehabilitation on the job. Many of the therapeutic strategies discussed in this chapter would be transferable to the workplace.

Notes

1   The information relating to cognitive rehabilitation is based on the work of Malia *et al.* (1997).

2   Cognitive behavioural therapy (CBT) needs to be distinguished from cognitive rehabilitation therapy (CRT).

Chapter 7

Enhancing Brain Functioning

While complete recovery can be achieved following the acquisition of a severe brain injury, there is a strong probability that the person will have to live and work with some degree of cognitive impairment. When no further improvement in cognitive ability can be expected, steps need to be taken to minimize the impact of any remaining deficit in their ability to carry out their everyday work and living skills. Managing or limiting the impact of cognitive problems is an essential element in returning the client to employment.

When cognitive function has been maximized and no further improvement can be expected, we need to turn to identifying measures that will reinforce and enhance natural cognitive aptitude. Nothing can replace the complexity and capability of our thought and reasoning processes, which evolved over millions of years. Aids, adaptations and strategies or the advice discussed in this chapter are designed to support existing brain structure but not to replace cognition.[1] Supportive mechanisms that work for one person can be off-putting to another. There is more likelihood of such tools being beneficial if the client's views and agreement are obtained prior to implementation of an enhancing strategy. A degree of trial and error is likely.

External aids and strategies

External aids that can enhance cognitive function include a daily diary, which can enhance memory by reminding individuals where they should be or what activity is planned. It can also act as a 'long-term memory' for past events. A notice board or post-its can be used in a prominent place to remind an individual of an intended activity or an important event that they are required to attend. Many modern mobile phones can be programmed to sound a signal and flash a pre-arranged text message, reminding an individual of necessary information or appointments.

External strategies can include workplace reorganization. Undertaken appropriately and with consideration, it can help to enhance cognitive functions such as memory. The broad principle of this type of adaptation is that the arrangement of the workstation and the work components are applied in a systematic way that assist rather than hinder memory. For example, if the job requires the construction of a computer monitor, lay out work components to be inserted into the computer monitor in a chronological order rather than a haphazard or flexible layout. This technique is more suitable for low-skilled employment than for work that requires a high degree of spontaneity. It also requires a degree of routine and familiarization with the job duties involved. External strategies are easier to use for this client group as they do not overload the already compromised cognitive skills.

Internal strategies

Internal strategies can also be applied to enhance memory functioning. Rehearsal of information involves repeating information over and over again until the person is confident that the information can be retained. A typical example of a rehearsal strategy in action is of an individual with visual/verbal memory problems, who cannot remember their colleague's names. The rehearsal strategy is to take photographs of the colleagues and write their names on the front of the photograph. It is best to ask the client to undertake this task as this helps build rapport. Systematically go over the photographs, asking the client to name the person in each photograph. As the client proves able to commit the names to memory, cover or partially cover them and repeat the process until the names have been learned. This is sometimes know as the errorless learning technique. It is a simple and successful method of learning names and faces. The PQRST technique (see Malia *et al.* 1997) is a systematic example of a rehearsal strategy. PQRST stands for:

- P (Preview) – Have the client read the information to obtain a flavour of what is involved.

- Q (Question) – Ask questions of the client in relation to the information.

- R (Read) – Read the information a second time to gain the answer to the questions you have raised.

- S (State) – Client states their answers.

- T (Test) – Check the validity of answers.

Mnemonics is another useful internal technique to be applied for retaining lists of information. This is the strategy used by card players when they are learning the position of hundreds of cards and can be quite impressive. One of the main advantages of this system is that the brain is not required to think verbally when it is trying to retrieve the information, but visually, which can make for a much stronger association. The secret (Berglas and Playfair 1988) is to weave a cartoon-like story that links each word to the next, using imagination and the power of visualization. From the list you need a central character around which you weave the story. A demonstration is provided below:

LIST = cat, book, wine, settee, table, orange

The *orange cat* was sitting by the *table*, drinking a glass of *wine*. He stood up and walked across to the *settee* and picked up an old *book*.

With this technique, it is essential that the individual create their own story, as this visually reinforces the information to be remembered. Mnemonics is a very effective strategy for learning lists of information or instructions and is worth persevering with. Unfortunately mnemonics can be off-putting for some people, who either prefer not to think visually or view it as a difficult strategy to implement. It would also be difficult for an individual who has damage to visual processing to successfully apply this method.

Inability or reduced ability to remember a sequence of numbers can be an associated problem of acquired brain injury. While it is perfectly feasible to write the number down, there are instances where we would not want to do this. We would not write down our security pin giving access to our banking details or security access to our office. Information is always much easier to remember if it has meaning attached. For example, a four-digit number is better remembered when separated and given a descriptor. This is also known as 'chunking'. The number 6734 will be better remembered as 67 people work on the 34th floor. This also enables the user to tap into visual information processing where possible.

A few individuals with an acquired brain injury lose all memories prior to their injury. They have no recollection of any childhood events, of parents, family or friends. Memories cannot be reformed if organic damage has occurred but information about their past can be relearned, through a type of biographical therapy. The basis of biographical therapy is to identify what information needs to be relearned and who would be the best person to approach to learn the information from. An example of this is tasking the client with asking a friend what teachers they had at school, or asking parents what employment they had undertaken or what educational qualifications they obtained. The PQRST technique described above can be useful in this regard. Biographical therapy can help the client make links and reconstruct relationships with friends and family they previously could not recall. This type of exercise is only for the clients with the severest retrograde amnesia. Not all clients falling into this category would want to participate in this and it is very much a personal choice of the individual, which needs to be respected. Some understandably would prefer to look forward and get on with the memories they do have the ability to recall.

Attention

Attention/concentration is one of the areas of cognitive damage that seem to improve most and where steps can be taken to minimize the impact on the workplace. I suspect one of the main reasons for the level of recovery in this area is that it is impossible to function day to day, without being exposed to stimuli requiring attention. It is this exposure (or practice) that promotes improvement. Attentional problems manifest in the workplace in a number of forms. Some clients will become engrossed in one particular aspect of the task. This may result in poor productivity, as the individual spends all of their time ensuring that a particular sub-task has been completed satisfactorily. Others may flit aimlessly between two or more tasks, failing to complete any of them.

Successful workplace performance requires obtaining a balance between quantity and quality of production. Cutting out irrelevant information in the workplace, where possible, can help to increase concentration, as can eliminating background noise. Setting clients appropriate work targets will ensure that they take into consideration quality of production and quantity of production. Set increasingly difficult tasks to work towards, record progress, and make positive contrasts between present and past performance. Concentration can be enhanced by incorporating frequent breaks into the work schedule.

Having the client undertake a task with which they are familiar is a double-edged sword in relation to enhancing attention. It promotes improvement where divided attention is an issue, but if the client is easily distracted, then a degree of variety is more stimulating and more likely to retain their attention.

Insight

It is one thing having cognitive problems and undertaking whatever steps you can to minimize the impact on work performance. It is quite another having no awareness or acceptance that a problem exists. Lack of insight into the cognitive difficulties affecting work performance can be a huge impediment to a successful workplacement. An individual who is unable to be aware or accept that their cognitive skill has been compromised would have no reason or incentive, as they saw it, to prescribe to strategies and methods to improve or assist functioning. Some individuals use denial of reduced ability as a defence mechanism. It is essential to understand that this differs from awareness problems. Denial is a psychological defence when something is perceived to be too painful to face up to. Lack of awareness is due to damage to those circuits in the brain that enable us to be aware.

It important not to rob clients of any hope that they have of recovering, particularly with clients who are suffering from depression, while at the same time remaining realistic. A good way to strike this balance is to talk about extended timescales for achievement rather than stating that they cannot be attained.

Although in brain injury rehabilitation and workplace reintegration it is generally advisable to focus on the positive, it is sometimes necessary to highlight where the client has performed poorly or where they have failed, if progress in other areas is to be made. Management of the problem should be both supportive and confronting of any difficulties that exist. Timing is essential. If the client is challenged too early in their recovery, they may be less inclined to be accepting of it or may well have emotional difficulty dealing with it.

Performance on the job is an ideal opportunity to increase the client's awareness of their own work-related performance and in what way cognitive impairment is impinging on certain skills. Clients should rate how they feel they will perform at a task. Following the completion of their work, their stated ability to undertake the task is rated with actual performance of the task. Discrepancies can be discussed at length, both in terms of quality and quantity of output. This in itself might be sufficient for them to realize they are not as skilled at the job duties as they view themselves or, for some, they are more able than they believe themselves to be.

Alternative methods include videotaping performance if appropriate, which can act as a useful feedback mechanism for identifying actual performance compared with the client's perceived performance. Inviting the client's colleagues to give feedback on how they have discharged their duties can in certain circumstances be effective, but should be undertaken with a great deal of sensitivity and, of course, with permission.

Executive skill

The setting of obtainable and realistic work goals is pretty much contingent on the extent of the client's executive skills. It is easy to understand the difficulties that might arise in the workplace if this type of ability is adversely affected. The client is likely to have the capability of undertaking only the most menial of work tasks. Carrying out menial jobs in the process of recovering will inevitably be frustrating and demeaning, particularly for clients who have held jobs at responsible levels.

The key to development enhancing executive skill is actual exposure to decision-making events. The client should work at the level they are capable of dealing with successfully, with a view to progressively increasing complexity. Their appeal for a work placement requiring greater responsibility and independence needs to be taken on board and dealt with empathetically, but nevertheless structured and monitored until they are capable of undertaking duties at such a level. Working in a structured setting indirectly keys the client into some of the decisions that have to be made, diminishing the client's need to plan and negating some of the need for lateral thinking. If progression is to be achieved, they need to be exposed to the mistakes they are making and training provided as to better practice. Competency exercises may be useful in this respect.

Literacy/numeracy

Most clients whose written communication skills have been affected express the fear that they are not intelligent any more, that they have lost their intellectual abilities. They also feel that they need to get everything perfect. If everything is not correct, they allow this to reinforce their feeling of failure and loss of their intelligence. Understandably, they will feel anxious when they have difficulty reading or writing. These are skills, after all, that they have performed for decades, on a daily basis without thought. Often the person will know how to execute a task, they can think it through, but the brain cannot put it into action. They know exactly what they wish to achieve, but the process of delivering this is difficult. Their reaction is to panic and when panic occurs the 'blinds' to improvement will come down.

A large part of what we are dealing with at this stage is the fundamental feelings of low self-esteem. Clients need to be reassured that they can recover and will improve, and for the vast majority, in relation to literacy and numeric skill, there will be progression. When small progress is achieved, the confidence and feeling of control that this generates acts as a catalyst for further recovery. When working on strategies to enhance work-related literacy or numeracy, the key objective is immediate success without being patronizing. This can be a difficult balance to achieve and involves providing training at their level of ability, but reassuring them that their performance is not reflective of their underlying intellectual capabilities. The skilled specialist will focus on the process of how the brain works and how memory, concentration and awareness fit into this process. Training in work-related literacy and numeric skills also needs to be related to workplace duties, and what the client wishes to achieve in terms of work.

Vision

Poor vision can make a work environment an extremely dangerous environment for the brain-injured employee. A good risk assessment can help to minimize this danger. Particular visual problems bring their own workplace difficulties and there needs to be a bespoke solution to compensate for the particular visual difficulty that the employee is having. For example, if the client has a left field visual neglect, placing work components to their right-hand side enables them to locate components without having to scan their workbench, increasing their ability to undertake work duties.

Psychological factors

Factors over and above cognitive damage can adversely impinge on cognitive functioning. Memory and attentional deficit, as an example, can be increased by psychological issues such as anxiety and confidence, and by the unfamiliarity of the situation in which the person now finds themselves. Anxiety is further increased by negative thinking, with clients often capitulating on a rehabilitation or a work task, without really trying. Negative thinking, if unchallenged, can lead to depression.

On the principle that psychological factors such as anxiety can adversely affect performance, it seems logical that cognitive functioning could be enhanced by the application of anxiety-reducing techniques such as yoga, breathing exercises or by formal counselling. In relation to reducing negative thinking and increasing confidence, identifying negative thoughts and writing down positive counter-arguments may bring about the appropriate balance of the person's capabilities. This is not denying that a problem exists but simply putting it in perspective.

Note

1   Aids, adaptations and strategies discussed in this chapter can also be used in conjunction with cognitive rehabilitation therapy discussed in the previous chapter. Strategies for enhancing cognitive function are used outside the therapeutic environment and often on a perm-anent basis, and therefore warrant a separate discussion.

Chapter 8

Occupational Techniques

Nothing is particularly hard if you divide it into small jobs.
Henry Ford, American industrialist

A number of occupational techniques borrowed and adapted from industry can be usefully employed to gather information in relation to the client, their abilities or what is involved in their work tasks. Information obtained can supplement occupational assessment and inform on vocational rehabilitation requirements, appropriate workplace strategies and workplace capabilities involved in putting people back into employment. Other techniques discussed in this chapter include motivational tools which can be used to good effect to maximize workplace performance, rehabilitation techniques and appropriate methods of supporting an individual who is struggling to undertake their work duties. This is by no means an exhaustive list nor is it intended as training in the techniques involved, but an acknowledgement that they exist to be exploited.

Information gathering
SWOT analysis

A SWOT analysis is a useful mechanism used within industry for gaining information. SWOT stands for Strengths, Weaknesses, Opportunities and Threats and is applied as a management development tool by occupational psychologists to obtain an overview of where an organization is currently operating at, and the future direction of the company. A SWOT analysis, in its organizational sense, is an internal survey of capabilities and an external review of society circumstances likely to impinge on the organization's success. As mentioned, it is usually undertaken on an organizational level but with a little thought can be adopted as a means of identifying the circumstances affecting the future of an individual.

In relation to an individual, a *strength* may be a transferable skill such as IT knowledge or knowledge of a foreign language. It can also be a personal attribute – friendly, outgoing, sociable etc. A weakness can be anything likely to hinder the person's success, but in a head-injured person may well be a function that has been adversely affected by cognitive injury. It may be poor written communication skill or poor motor control, for example. Personal attributes can also be a weakness if they affect workplace performance. Clients may feel that they are stubborn, shy, lazy or a whole host of other negatives that might impinge on their employment potential. Weaknesses identified can be categorized as pre-injury and post-injury.

Opportunities are described as the prospects that are available to an organization, or in this instance to an individual. Financial compensation as a consequence of an injury could be viewed as an opportunity to open that small shop on the sea front or the pub that they always aspired to. No longer being able to undertake physical activity from which they have always earned their living might open up opportunities to retrain in telephone sales, which they have been considering for many years.

Threats can be identified as any barrier to successful return to employment. Facing discrimination as a disabled person or a memory problem limiting job prospects are examples of this. Alternatively it may be a downturn in the job market, which results in more difficulty finding employment.

To undertake a SWOT analysis requires you to give the client four pieces of paper each with the heading of each of the following: Strengths, Weaknesses, Opportunities or Threats. Ask them to complete the sheets, which you then analyse and discuss with the client.

Information from a SWOT analysis can be used to formulate strategies. It helps in the decision-making process and helps establish an overall picture. It is a relatively fast and efficient method of exploring possibilities and expanding a client's vocational vision.

An individual SWOT analysis is a highly subjective exercise but the purpose is to start to build and develop a foundation of where the client is now, and the career direction they could possibly travel towards in the future. The findings are not set in concrete but can change and develop as the client recovers and increases in confidence and aspiration. It can be used as a means of opening up new possibilities. In SWOT analysis it is imperative that the person themselves identifies the strengths, weaknesses, opportunities and threats. The individual needs to be practical about their own assets and potential shortfalls. In identifying strengths and weaknesses, it can be helpful to obtain the perspective of a spouse/friend/colleague to provide an objective sounding board.

If nothing else, a SWOT analysis is a holistic overview and in-depth insight of how your clients are viewing themselves. It also provides an opportunity to raise and discuss issues if they are unrealistic, overambitious or underambitious.

Job analysis

Whereas SWOT analysis is a useful tool to identify information about the client, a useful resource that can be used to obtain information about the requirements of a particular occupation is job analysis. Job analysis enables identification of the components of tasks and the environment in which the work is being carried out, permitting the identification of potential areas of difficulties in which the client will need particular support.[1] Job analysis identifies a number of crucial aspects of a job within the work environment.

Job analysis is a method historically developed and used by occupational psychologists to gather information about work competencies and requirements for a job. This information would then be used to form a job description to ensure that the potential employee has the skill specification. Traditionally, it has enabled the employer to identify the appropriate criteria by which to assess a potential employee. It can also be used to identify training requirements, future needs, promotions as well as satisfy legal requirements that employers are not discriminating against disabled people.

Job analysis is undertaken in a structured manner to ensure that every element of the job is fully understood. When undertaking a job analysis, information should be gained from a number of valid sources rather than just one source. A combination of various analytical information-gathering methods are used including structured questionnaires and interviews, which attempt to break a particular job down to its constituent parts, looking at the various skills, strengths and capabilities required to successfully carry out the work. Structured questions can be used to identify exactly what competencies are required for a person to successfully carry out their work role. Other information which may be useful includes appropriate employer's documentation, such as a job description. Alternatively, a current job holder can be asked to maintain a diary for a specific period, perhaps three weeks to ensure that a wide range of the job requirements are identified. The length of time required to maintain the diary would depend very much on the complexity of the job. Each work role is unique and it is not appropriate for information obtained from one position to be transferred to another job role.

In relation to returning a brain-injured individual back to employment, job analysis should identify the actual subtask or tasks involved in a work role. It should also identify the physical and cognitive requirements of each subtask, enabling the identification of potential areas the client is likely to have difficulty with.

Repertory grid interview

Repertory grid was developed by a psychologist called Kelly in the 1950s. It was developed to identify the common viewpoint (or constructs) in evaluation of a product or person's performance. Kelly developed this technique to elicit and assess the relationships between personal constructs (Kelly 1955).

Repertory grid can be undertaken in relation to a product or in relation to a job performance. Respondents are provided with elements in groups of three and asked to think of a way in which two of the elements differ from the third. This would naturally identify its opposite. For example, two of the elements may be long while one is short. In this instance length has been identified as a measurable concept. Managers are asked to identify the skills and attributes that make people successful in a particular role. They achieve this by identifying three job holders and explaining how two of them differ from the third in how they execute their duties. This is continued until an appropriate amount of attributes, measuring successful performance, has been identified.

In relation to returning brain-injured people to employment, repertory grid can be used to ensure that their abilities match core job requirements. It enables identification of categories of a task by which individual employees differ and what would be required for acceptable and competent performance.

Critical incident technique

Often when a job is low skilled, the requirements are self-evident. This is not the case when an individual has undertaken a job with a high degree of complexity such as that expected in a professional or managerial position. In this instance, the skill involved is not always tangible. Critical incident technique can help to identify some of the more subtle skills involved in higher level management, by exploring real events which have actually occurred in the job. This technique was developed by John Flanagan as a means of identifying competencies/behaviour that would make someone successful in a particular job (Flanagan 1954).

Critical incident technique is used to identify behaviours that influence success or failure in a work situation. Basically it involves asking work colleagues who undertake a similar role to that of your client, to identify a couple of critical incidents which occurred in the course of undertaking their job duties, identifying which tasks they had dealt with successfully and which tasks were not dealt with well. These critical incidents are then explored in greater depth to identify which behavioural traits were in evidence and which skills were used to cope adequately with the incidents that occurred. It will also identify which skills were lacking in the poorer performances.

Critical incident technique can be used with a brain-injured employee after a period of work reintegration, to identify which higher-level tasks they are coping with well and which they have had difficulty with. Having identified the skills the client is not performing very well, appropriate rehabilitation or training can be organized to enhance these skills. As poor insight can be an issue with a brain-injured person, the presence of a colleague or manager when gaining this information would help to ensure that the information being provided is indeed an accurate reflection of performance.

Task analysis

Task analysis is an information-giving tool used by ergonomics and occupational psychology. Task analysis allows highly structured understanding of a particular task, breaking it down to its component parts to allow a more systematic and logical understanding of how a task is accomplished. Analysis of individual elements can be undertaken within the context of the whole task, which allows various levels of detail to be reviewed. The main remit of task analysis is to evaluate the interactions between user and a work machine or system, and to design jobs taking into account the person's limitations and capabilities. Nevertheless it has a number of other potential applications including training, workload assessment, identifying operator support and workplace redesign. It can be used, with a little adaptation, to support changing requirements in user-machine interface, for those individuals returning to employment following an injury. Task analysis has the potential to ensure safe and efficient machine usage by clients returning to work with cognitive deficit, following an acquired brain injury.

There are three main steps to task analysis and I refer the reader to Salvendy (1987) for a fuller description. The first step is identifying and gathering information about the requirement of the task, reducing this to subtasks. The second step involves recording appropriate data. Various formats can be used for recording information and will very much depend on the task involved. The final step is to analyse your information. There are various techniques for this analysis, dependent upon a number of issues including how complex you require the analysis to be.

Training needs analysis

A training needs analysis will enable you to identify where training is needed and help you align this with organizational goals and culture. It also helps you identify potential workplace hazards and general health and safety implications.

Ongoing motivational support

Mentoring

The above mentioned occupational techniques are methods of gathering information, to enable identification of appropriate rehabilitation and training strategies, to meet potential shortfalls in a client's capabilities. Mentoring is a process of ongoing support for an individual, through a difficult period in their work. Such systems are currently widely used in organizations, for the development of young managers who are new to a job. Mentoring can involve a variety of workplace assistance, from shadowing a colleague to confiding in them work-related problems. The essence of successful mentoring is ensuring that the individual, who is all too often lacking in experience hence also confidence, feels comfortable approaching the mentor for guidance and support.

The mentoring system could easily be adapted to benefit the brain-injured client as a supportive structure over the medium to long term, helping the individual reintegrate back into the workplace. A mentor in this situation should be a colleague who can help keep a supportive eye on the client. The mentor should preferably be a colleague who knows all areas of the client's job. The mentor in this situation could also help the individual with decisions, help with guidance, workplace support and provide an established communication link to other parts of the organization. Before the mentoring process begins, the client's personal needs, their requirements and their expectations would be identified. This would include identifying their fears, strengths and weaknesses.

The expectations of a mentor are that they are approachable, that they should maintain confidentiality, be enthusiastic, experienced and respected in their work role. Ideally they will be good at motivating others, someone the client feels comfortable confiding in and who has the time to commit to the process. The mentor should not have any managerial responsibility for the person, should avoid making promises that they are not in a position to fulfil and should not become personally involved. The mentee should have equal input into how the relationship is to be conducted. Consequently the nature of the relationship between mentor and mentee should be open to negotiation from the start. Boundaries and expectations need to be identified and put in place, otherwise one side (or both) may feel let down. Both parties should have responsibilities within the relationship. If the mentoring process continues when the client feels it is no longer necessary, it may well be detrimental to progression. Consequently when the client feels they have made sufficient progress, they need to be encouraged to end the mentoring process in a positive way. Steps to end the mentoring arrangement can be formalized at the initial setting of boundaries and expectations.

Goal setting

Goal setting is an occupational technique which can increase motivation. Goal (target) setting can be used to motivate a client, as it can divide complex tasks into more manageable segments. It is also designed to raise skill level and increase self-confidence. The key to success is setting goals at an appropriate level. If the target is too easy, it can lead to poor results, poor motivation and can be subconsciously interpreted by the client as not having confidence in their ability. Conversely, if goals are set too high, failure to achieve the set goals invariably ends with the client becoming irritable at their own poor performance. Sometimes the response is to become angry with themselves and then dismiss the task as unachievable, setting the client back in terms of confidence, motivation and progress. Targets should be reachable but challenging without putting the client in a pass or fail situation. The client needs to have some ownership and be involved in identifying the targets. Involving the client in setting the goals can serve as a motivator for them to build up output over a period of time. There is little value in setting outcomes which are dependent on factors outside the client's control.

To provide a degree of structure and expectation, it is generally better to assign a time frame to the goals. Long-term, medium-term and short-term goals will suffice. Goals need to be specific rather than vague. They should also be stated in positive terms. Goals need to have purpose and meaning to the individual undertaking them or they are unlikely to psychologically ascribe to them. While working towards their goals, clients benefit from genuinely accurate feedback, ensuring that the individual is well aware of difficulties in their performance. This should be coupled with suggestions in how to overcome any problems that have emerged. Honest, constructive feedback will help to increase performance. The workplace mentor can take responsibility for this feedback.

Small, achievable but challenging goals should be set which will enable employers to gauge how much progress has been made and possibly give some indication of how much improvement might be expected. As activities become routine, more complexity can be added and a range of different targets progressively built into a daily or weekly planner. Clients need to persevere with tasks in which they are slow, which they find frustrating or embarrassing, as these difficulties need to be faced, either to be conquered, or accepted as unachievable at which point set less demanding goals and pay the matter no further attention.

Subdivide specific tasks identified as goals, asking the client to rate how well they feel that they can undertake each element. This provides additional measures of their ability to reach the goals being set. Line managers can rate actual performance with expected performance and discuss differences with their employee. Group goal setting, which can be undertaken within a rehabilitation setting, can foster interpersonal skill, team working and agreement where this has been an area identified as requiring development.

Competency exercises

As mentioned in Chapter 2, competency exercises are ideal for vocational rehabilitation, as a means of training individuals in areas in which they have difficulty but which are essential for successful performance of their job (see Chapters 5 and 6). This enables practice of the skill to be undertaken, but without risk, should mistakes be made. Identification of the necessary competences required can be achieved using some of the methods explained in this section. Having identified appropriate competences for a number of clients, exercises should be generated that replicate the necessary skills. Group assessment centres could be set up with a view to developing rather than assessing the skill. A development centre may be a more appropriately label. Feeding back to the clients good practice and poor practice, and allowing peer group reviews, can be an excellent method of enlightening and developing interactive skills and executive skills of brain-injured individuals.

Final thoughts

Some of the occupational tools and methods discussed in this chapter are highly specialized and a practitioner is likely to obtain more from their client and their situation if they are competent and experienced in their use. The reader should seek further training, should they wish to adopt these occupational techniques as part of their skill base. Alternatively they should appoint an appropriately qualified occupational professional experienced in using the above mentioned methods.

Note

1   Information relating to job analysis is adapted from *Guidelines for Best Practice in the Use of Job Analysis Techniques* by SHL Groups plc (2001).

Chapter 9

Workplace Reintegration

Work is nature's best physician and central to human happiness.
Claudius Galen, 1772

Two distinct categories of acquired brain injury exist in relation to returning to the workplace: those with long-established brain injury who have not worked for many years and those who have relatively recently acquired their injury. Recent brain injury can for employment purposes be defined as those individuals whose cognitive functioning is still improving, around two years post-injury or less.

Long-established injury

With long-term brain injury, there is every prospect that barriers to employment will be psychological as much as cognitive or physical in nature and may include such factors as self-confidence, enthusiasm and career direction. Unless they have severe cognitive problems which self-evidently rule them out of undertaking work tasks, it can be difficult to predict the prospects of occupational success, without a work trial of considerable length. A work trial will give the client the opportunity to improve and develop as much as they can in a supportive environment. It enables the client to practise their skills and ascertain their capacity to return to employment. It also provides the opportunity for the client to prove themselves capable of undertaking work duties.

Initially, when returning the client with long-established brain injury to the workplace, it is best to seek employment where there is limited executive functioning required, or where there is not a great deal of variation to the routines of the job, regardless of levels of employment they attained prior to their injury. It is more productive to proceed with tasks that do not have a high demand for accuracy. Brain-injured clients often focus a great deal on accuracy to the detriment of speed, only to then become frustrated with the low quantity of production.

Recent brain injury

Clients returning to work after many years will inevitably have low confidence, which can be difficult to restore. This, however, contrasts with the outlook of the recently brain-injured client who will all too often be overly enthusiastic, overly confident, and out to prove to themselves and others that they can function as well as before. Unfortunately they rarely have the cognitive skills to match. It can be difficult for this group to accept emotionally their limitations on ability and they often hold the view that they will make a full recovery. It is almost as important not to squash this enthusiasm as it is not to promote false hope. A gradual return to work in line with the client's capabilities is recommended, rather than following their own enthusiasm which is often based on judgement impaired as a consequence of their injury.

Regardless of the length of time the individual has lived with an acquired brain injury, those who do return to work often fail to rise above the first basic routine job that the job coach or employment adviser has secured for them. The approach to date is viewed as employing them 'out of harm's way'. Thankfully this attitude is slowly changing as organizations realize that this disabled group is capable of much more challenging work. Experience has demonstrated that failure on one occasion does not necessarily imply that the client will fail in a subsequent attempt. The main principle in returning clients to employment following acquired brain injury is to keep development opportunities open for them. Clients should be encouraged to push for small successes and their abilities stretched until they have reached their maximum employment level. Individuals should concentrate on the tasks that they can do well, but with a view to developing the skills that they are not so good at. It is essential that the client accepts that it is not where they start in their return to employment that is important, but where they finish.

Inevitably there will be some reduction of employment prospects for individuals with acquired brain injury. Individuals who undertook manual work prior to injury, generally will have an easier time returning to employment, because their work can often be less cognitively demanding. Managers and graduates whose responsibilities require abstract analysis, dealing with numerous tasks simultaneously and dealing with the unexpected, find it more difficult when returning to employment. Long-term prospects remain poor at this stage. Professionals, who have a large store of knowledge which is lost because of retrograde memory problems, are likely to have great difficulty returning to their former career. Initially it can be difficult for the managerial/professional group to cross the psychological chasm, to undertake duties that offer less responsibility and prestige than that enjoyed prior to the injury, but unless a full cognitive recovery is made, a less demanding role usually needs to be accepted if they are to succeed in their return to employment.

Job retention

When returning to employment following brain injury, it is easier to return to a current employer than to look for new employment. The client's existing workplace is likely to provide the necessary ingredients for successful reintegration back into their job, including familiarity, stability, friendship and support. The government has encouraged a number of job retention schemes which will support this as an option.

One exception to the client returning to their original workplace as soon as possible is when a son or daughter works for their parents, in which case subtle dependency bonds are likely to inhibit recovery. In these circumstances, the brain-injured client could benefit from moving away from the protective environment of their parents' business for a period of six months to one year. This will help circumvent the parent-child dynamics and the natural parental concern and inclination to overprotect and indulge them as a dependent child. This gives the brain-injured client the opportunity to increase their work discipline and to push themselves until they reach their work potential.

Brain-injured people very much focus on their label of their disability, as can their work colleagues. A common experience of brain-injured clients returning to their former workplace is for well-meaning colleagues who know the type of injury that has been sustained, to communicate their expectations (albeit be it subtly and without malice) for him or her to be unable to function as they once did. The client is under no obligation to meet low anticipation of their future success. More sinister is the colleague who will allow their own poor performance to be attributed to the brain-injured employee, who all to often is not in a position to defend their work output.

Employer rapport

The employer and other employees of a company will know the job duties that have to be undertaken, much better than anyone else involved with the client, including the case manager or whoever is responsible for their return to work. Where possible, involve colleagues in identifying job requirements and finding solutions to overcome potential problems. This has the added advantage of building workplace rapport with the employer and helping the client feel more confident in undertaking job duties. Methods of identifying workplace requirements are discussed in the previous chapter.

Establishing a good relationship with your client's employer as early as possible has advantages. It enables you to educate the employer on the general problems associated with brain injury and the idiosyncratic limitations of the particular client you are working with. Profile strengths and weaknesses of your client and prepare the employer for what to expect. Involve the employer as fully as you can in the work-related rehabilitation process and in any decisions or events that encroach on the employer's time, such as case conferences, future challenges, development plan etc. The client nevertheless should not be made to feel secondary in decisions/ events that are principally about them. Pre-accident and post-accident comparisons, although initially helpful, soon become wearing. Employers will often say that so-and-so is not the same employee, usually referring to a task the client could perform better prior to the injury. The employer needs to accept that their employee is very often not the same employee they once had and should work with the person he or she currently is.

Mistakes

Errors of judgement will inevitably occur and should be dealt with sensitively. Criticism is likely to discourage the client from trying. There can be a tendency for line managers to either be overcritical if they feel overall output is diminished because they are required to support an employee, or understate the extent of the real problems to protect the client's feelings. Clients should be confronted with mistakes if improvements are to be made but this must be undertaken in an empathetic and supportive manner. Highlight what the client can do well and what can be achieved with a bit of support, but not by downplaying their difficulties.

We all err in our work performance, consequently mistakes should not be automatically attributed to a brain injury, either by the client or their employer. An individual with a brain injury is unfortunately always under the microscope, with various people from human resources to rehabilitation staff, trying to identify mistakes in work performance. This heightened sensitivity can have a detrimental effect on the client's confidence and their self-belief system with regards to their work duties. Such intrusion is something few of us would or could tolerate and if it did occur, errors in our own performance would not only emerge, but in all likelihood increase as our concentration became adversely affected by anxiety and concern. Brain-injured people can be overconscious about mistakes that non-brain-injured people would not acknowledge or, if it was acknowledged, would attribute to tiredness or boredom. We need to consider carefully if it is a brain error or a human error. A good rule of thumb is a brain error will occur again and again after being highlighted. An everyday human error should not be repeated, if the employee is being more vigilant against the error.

Job security

Job security is a common element considered important by brain-injured clients. This is partially due to their vulnerability and the difficulty that they can face finding another job, and partially related to decreased self-esteem. It may also be difficult to establish friendships if they moved to a new job and they do not wish to have this to deal with on top of everything else. Additionally the client may have some indication that their behaviour in some situations is unacceptable and, in less supportive circumstances, this may result in them losing their job.

Supported employment

There are a number of government employment initiatives which can help brain-injured clients return to employment. The supported placement scheme is designed to assist people with a disability, who are registered as disabled, to enter or return to employment. Under this programme, people who are medically fit to work but unable to function to full capacity in the workplace may have part of their salary funded by the government. This can help ease people with a brain injury back into work, as employers may be more willing to offer employment when they are not financially responsible for the shortfall between an individual's level of efficiency/output and their salary. However, in practice, funding for this type of activity is limited and there can be a waiting period to participate in the scheme. Further information about access to supported employment or other government initiatives is obtainable through the Disability Employment Adviser (DEA) at the local Jobcentreplus office.

Timing the return to work

Timing is essential for successful reintegration of brain-injured people into the workplace. Too soon a return to the workplace, when the client is not sufficiently recovered, is likely to result in loss of confidence, with the person becoming demoralized. Too late a return and the optimum opportunity for maximum workplace reintegration has been missed. The appropriate time to return to employment is not an easy decision and should be based on the severity of injury, level of recovery, the type of work duties required, the level of support available, client insight and the degree of co-operation from the employer.

In order to prosper, the client needs a work environment that is supportive while at the same time it stretches and develops them. The ideal environment should afford the opportunity to put their capabilities to the test and to learn from their mistakes. They also need to be encouraged to persevere through inevitable setbacks and frustration, not to mention mistakes, if they are to make a successful transition into employment. With more severely brain-injured clients, the case manager needs to establish that they can be left without supervision. Employment duties that an employee undertakes will need to have a degree of flexibility, to allow for fluctuations in their stamina and pain levels incurred while performing work duties. Frequent rest periods should be built in to their work schedule.

In the longer term, the employment professional should aim towards providing a challenging work environment that encourages the client to ruminate and make decisions, rather than an environment that simply keeps them occupied or enables them to 'switch off' while working. This will eventually entail variety and graded complexity in line with capabilities. When the complexity of work tasks progresses to the next level, they may require further on-the-job support.

Task ownership is essential in successful work reintegration. When sufficient development/recovery has occurred, clients should be given responsibility for organizing and seeing through to the end, small-scale events as a training technique and to encourage acceptance of more responsibility. This can also help to increase confidence. Should this prove successful, the scale and size of responsibilities should be increased until the individual has reached their potential. Give the client control over the speed of output, gently motivating them by setting targets to increase their speed. Ensure the client is involved in setting the targets. In the longer term, the client needs to accept responsibility for their own success.

Emotional and psychological issues

Prevent the client from dwelling on what they cannot do. This can only be demotivating and detrimental. The employee would benefit from being encouraged to focus energy on their abilities, rather than inabilities, concentrating on what they can achieve. Some clients, when faced with minor difficulties, panic, preferring to ask for guidance and further support, rather than working through the problem to reach a solution themselves. An employee involved in the decision-making process is much more likely to retain skills or instructions, than the passive recipient of decisions made for them. Let the client work through problems themselves where possible and come to their own conclusions. A helping hand can be given by questioning them on what they believe should happen, given the situation. This will help to empower the brain-injured client to take simple workplace decisions that can all too often be difficult for them. The level of decision making can be increased as and when they prove capable and confident of dealing with more complex situations.

Identifying what the client considers will be the most difficult aspect of their job helps to identify where their workplace anxieties are likely to be placed. Once identified, this can become an area for special consideration and support. If they can master this issue, it will increase their confidence in dealing with the other employment tasks involved in their job.

Clients quickly become frustrated at not being able to undertake simple work tasks. As mentioned above, they concentrate so much on what they cannot do that they fail to appreciate the great amount they have achieved. There can be a tendency to create their own pressure because of a need to accomplish a task with perfection, regarding everything as a test and invariably comparing themselves with how they would have performed prior to the sustained injury. Anything short of perfection is considered confirmation of their perceived uselessness.

The more tense and frustrated an individual is, the more difficult tasks are to complete, even the most simple of tasks. The employment professional needs to find a way of relaxing their client and convincing them to accept that errors are going to be made and that this is not an indication of failure but perhaps down to anxiety, frustration or an unrealistic drive for perfection. Regardless of the reason a mistake occurs, it needs to be viewed as a positive part of the rehabilitation and relearning process.

Establishing and maintaining social contact requires higher cognitive skill and is of particular concern in workplace reintegration. Promotion at work is inextricably linked to good social skills and having social support within the workplace. Despite initial goodwill and genuine attempts by colleagues to help where possible, when an individual has suffered a brain injury, they can only too often become isolated in their workplace. The client is in danger of finding themselves cut off and without support. The difficulties usually lie with the client, who fails to initiate or respond to genuine attempts from others to develop work-related friendships. Colleagues often give up trying to build relationships or re-establish friendships within a few weeks or months of the individual either returning to their existing job or starting a new workplacement. Drifting into isolation in the workplace needs to be addressed, particularly if it was not a pre-injury personality trait. Employers should be encouraged, where possible, to go out of their way to include the client and to make them feel part of the team.

Motivation

Motivation can be a major factor in the successful return to employment for brain-injured clients. Most have an abundance of enthusiasm and are highly motivated and determined to return to some form of employment, which can be harnessed and channelled. As mentioned previously, some clients may be overenthusiastic, fully believing that they can return to their old self and determined to return to employment at the level they enjoyed pre-injury. However, if allowed to attempt to return to employment at a level beyond their capabilities, they will ultimately fail, which will increase their sense of despondency.

Motivation issues can be psychological in origin or as a direct result of the damage to the brain, leading to a state of not having any drive or not caring. Often there is a combination of both. Where it does prove difficult to motivate a client, they are more likely to attempt tasks that are relatively short in duration and where the individual can see an end goal in sight, rather than a constant continuation of an endless, monotonous task. Larger tasks should be divided into stages of shorter duration. Regular breaks, variety where possible and a reward system of some description are essential to encourage the client to participate. When a timetable of activity has been established, it soon becomes a routine norm rather than additional activity for the client to endure.

Mild injury

Any mild knock to the head, with accompanying symptoms, warrants attention and possibly supportive interaction from human resources or a case manager, to provide support through this period of difficulty. This will give long-term benefits to the client who will retain their job and savings to the company who will not be required to fund the cost of recruiting and retraining another employee. Many difficulties can be averted by providing appropriate education about the symptoms, natural course of recovery and what can be done to compensate in the meantime. If the problem persists, professional help should be sought.

Health and safety

Throughout this book I have emphasized and highlighted that health and safety is paramount in returning brain-injured people back into the workplace. Too often, however, it can be a convenient excuse not to employ a disabled person. 'Health and safety' is a phrase that has required no further explanation, impossible to argue against. Regardless of who is undertaking a job, whether they have a disability or not, there is always an element of risk involved. In relation to employing brain-injured people, however, it should be about identifying and managing risks, not eliminating them. Sensible precautions need to be in place but all employers will be expected to make reasonable adjustments to their workplace to accommodate a brain-injured individual. Failure to do so or hiding behind health and safety issues will contravene Disability Discrimination Legislation. In relation to work reintegration and health and safety in particular, employers should not be making assumptions about the brain-injured employee's capabilities.

They are not competent to make such judgements. Employers should at least be committed to flexible working arrangements, ensuring all staff are aware of the company's commitment to disabled people, providing training opportunities and where possible solving problems that may arise such as transport.

Nevertheless good judgement and common sense does need to be applied and an appropriate balance needs to be achieved. There are many genuine health and safety risks in the workplace, and advice and guidance are provided for good reason. There will be certain occupations where clients with cognitive problems would have great difficulty returning, particularly aspects of the health profession where the distribution of advice and medication can have catastrophic consequences for members of the public or where there is such potential danger to the client or to others that trial and error learning would be unacceptable. Each client's circumstances and the risks that their job poses to themselves and to others need to be reviewed on an individual basis. Clients are usually realistic about what would be appropriate.

Disability Discrimination Act

The Disability Discrimination Act (DDA) 1995 legislated against discrimination of disabled people. It is unlawful for employers to discriminate against potential job applicants or existing employees for a reason relating to their disability, if they are capable of undertaking their work duties. This includes individuals who have acquired a brain injury. The Act covers all areas of employment including promotion, selection, training and dismissal. In addition, it requires schools and institutes of further and higher education to provide appropriate information. The DDA defines a disability as a physical or mental impairment which has a substantial and long-term adverse impact on an individual's ability to undertake a normal day's work activity.

Employers are under an obligation to undertake reasonable adjustments to enable the disabled person to obtain or retain employment. Employers do have the right to ask if an individual has a disability or health problem prior to a job interview, if it is likely to affect their ability to perform their work duties. A job candidate has a duty to tell a potential employer about a disability, if it is likely to present as a difficulty in the workplace or present as a safety risk to themselves or others. Failure to do so may lead to dismissal at a later stage. The employer cannot make a reasonable adjustment to the workplace, if they are not aware of an employee's disability.

Driving

Reduced cognitive problems, impaired vision or increased possibility of epilepsy results in added dangers to driving following the acquisition of a brain injury. This is a particular problem if driving a heavy goods vehicle (HGV) or public service vehicle (PSV) which has the potential for greater damage, but additional caution is required of drivers of all vehicle types. Following a brain injury, individuals are required to surrender their driving licence. They are under a duty to inform the driver's medical unit at the Driving and Vehicle Licensing Authority (DVLA). If the person has never driven before their accident and would like to learn, they are obliged to disclose any sustained brain injury to the licensing authorities. Failure to inform the authorities may invalidate their insurance and lead to criminal prosecution. The medical advisor from the DVLA will write to ask the client permission to contact their GP.

Before the individual is allowed to return to driving, the DVLA may well require that they sit a driving assessment to ascertain their suitability to return to the road. This requirement makes good sense. The driving assessment is designed to focus on the skills needed to drive safely and this may include peripheral vision, cognitive and perceptual skills, following instructions, pain level experienced, reaction time, observational skill, ability to interpret complex road situations, dealing simultaneously with competing information, the ability to judge speed, distance and depth and general road awareness. As mentioned the standard for HGV and PSV drivers is likely to be higher than for drivers of ordinary vehicles.

Following the assessment, the driving centre prepares a report putting forward their recommendation of the person's suitability to drive. The following categories can be given:

1. not competent to drive

2. competent to drive

3. competent to drive but required to undertake retraining and re-familiarization.

Should they fall into the latter category, the assessor may well suggest a driving school that will specialize in providing the type of retraining that the individual needs. The medical authority at DVLA may ask the individual concerned to apply for a provisional disability driving licence, to enable them to undertake whatever recommendations have been suggested, before a reassessment at a later stage.

Regardless of their performance at this assessment, the medical examiner at DVLA has final veto in relation to the person having their driving licence returned to them. The medical examiner will take a whole host of issues into consideration when making their judgement. The person may feel they performed well in their assessment, but still not be reissued with their driving license. Decisions can be appealed against within six months, should they choose to do so.

Chapter 10

Case Studies

Not waving but drowning.

Stevie Smith

To successfully support an individual with cognitive deficits back into employment, it is essential that you have some insight and sensitivity to their experiences and how this has shaped them as the person now before you. The typical feelings of anger, fear, resentment and aloneness can be intensified when the individual is at the stage of returning to work, as the trials and tribulations of this final hurdle set new and increasingly demanding challenges, either to be achieved successfully or to be acknowledged as unattainable, enabling them to move on to activity that is within their ability.

I have included a number of case studies in this book. The aim of the case studies is not to demonstrate good practice. Indeed, some of the information within this chapter may contradict the good practice I have discussed previously. Nor is this chapter about successful transition into employment. Although positive outcomes can be achieved, the experiences of the individuals portrayed in this chapter have generally been negative. The intention is to provide the reader with some insight into the often overlooked emotional rollercoaster that the client will have experienced in their journey back to employment, enabling the practitioner to interact more empathetically with their client.

All the case studies included in this chapter are both factual and typical of the experiences of acquired brain injury of such severity that vocational rehabilitation was required. Identities are nevertheless disguised to protect confidentiality. The personal journeys are recalled in the client's style of communication. I have not attempted to structure it in any way or to interpret meaning, nor have I asked them to focus on employment. The reader may identify a number of common themes, but this is coincidental. The idea is to let the client put forward what is important to them, giving at least some voice to the group most affected by brain injury.

Of particular emphasis however, in all the discussions I have had, is the 'unrealness of their new world and detachment from the human race. Like stepping into another planet never experienced'.[1] From discussion with various people who have acquired a brain injury, I have formed the impression that the experience is akin to travelling alone to a completely alien civilization, where you read up on the culture before you travel, but reading the story does not quite prepare you for the reality of what you find when you go there.

Samantha

As with most people who have acquired a brain injury, Samantha was determined to return to her job as a manager trainee as soon as possible after her injury. In retrospect, she feels that the biggest mistake was trying to return to work too soon. She felt that the other big mistake she made was not admitting to herself or to others when things went wrong. Looking back, she felt ashamed at not having the courage to confess that she was not coping and to ask for help and assistance. She tried to be too independant in managing her condition and she wished someone had impressed upon her the severity of her situation. Although off work for a year, when she returned to her job, Samantha attempted to treat her brain injury as if she had caught a cold. 'Yes, I had a major injury but I'm fine now.'

When she returned to her employer, Samantha was not placed back on the project that she was working on prior to her injury. That project had long finished and her peers had moved on to other activities. This was never explained to her but the penny eventually dropped some weeks later. In trying to identify where things went wrong in returning to her job, she cites this experience as one of those points that seemed trivial but nevertheless important. It somehow made her feel that everything had moved on while her life had remained static. 'I had fallen off the merry-go-round.'

She was given a different job with colleagues who did not know her. She had been shy and reticent prior to her injury but more so following the injury. It was impossible to establish relationships with her new colleagues; they were so closed to her. She felt that she stuck out like a sore thumb. She felt squeezed out. She at least was convinced of her capabilities. She was an intelligent woman, a graduate. Admittedly she was stubborn, bordering on arrogant when it came to her views about her intellectual capabilities. Nevertheless she was aware that something was wrong and that somehow she was living a lie. She could not put her finger on it. It took her a long time to realize that there was a problem. She did not want to believe it.

Thinking back on it, she feels that her colleagues almost certainly knew she had acquired a brain injury. Nevertheless she went to tremendous efforts to try and hide this from them, almost as if she had committed a crime. Partly she was embarrassed, feeling it was a stigma that set her apart as abnormal. She felt that other people would look down on her and not involve her in activities. They did not include her anyway; her social life with colleagues, which was never brilliant, disappeared altogether. She felt stigmatized in the same way that people with a mental health problem are made to feel. 'They did not understand.' Invariably she tried to prove to herself and others that nothing was wrong, 'fought for normality', but the more that she tried, the more it seemed to reinforce the view of others.

Samantha tried hard to fit into the organization but felt it was very much her versus the employer. A 'them and me' sort of attitude existed and there were a lot more of them. She describes a climate of fear. They could score endless goals against her but she could not score, the goal posts would have moved. The human resources department were of no help, generally taking the side of the employer rather than being neutral. More surprisingly, her union supported her employer. Any suggested advances or a way forward always had a health and safety objection applied to it.

Samantha found a number of things particularly frustrating. Top of the list was the degradation of getting all the rubbish jobs. She describes not challenging her employer on being given menial jobs as a further mistake on her part. She had always felt that the jobs she was given were well below her capabilities, yet she always struggled to finish the projects. She was also asked to find her own workplacements within the company, which given her unpopularity, creating an additional strain. She describes herself scrambling around like an eager puppy, trying to cajole some manager into letting her join their team. Gaining a placement had been made more difficult, because she had been formally disciplined for her poor throughput of work. She accepts that her performance was undoubtedly less than she would have expected from herself. She reports that she felt her 'engine' speed was not up to it. She did not have the courage to confide in her employer, for fear of prejudicing her ability to keep her job.

The mechanisms used by her employer to help actually hindered her. This included the training/learning technique of being moved from project to project every few weeks. This meant that she was not able to consolidate tasks or build relationships with colleagues. Discussions of progress from professional support was aimed at the management, almost excluding her. Eventually the meetings were held without her. Counselling was available through human resources, but 'How could they understand? What could they do? What understanding and support could they possibly provide?'

She felt singled out by an unfair regime. Her difficult situation was made psychologically impossible by an unthinking and uncaring employer, who only ever relayed negative information about her performance. When the company that employed her made a statement that they were looking to make people redundant, she feared the worst. She describes the closing stages of her employment as a haze of fog and a feeling of fighting to keep afloat, almost certainly due to the depression that was engulfing her. She was handed a letter: her job was gone. A graduate medically retired at 28 years of age.

Samantha feels that acquiring a brain injury has made her grow up quicker in the way that a major confrontation with life does. It also made her realize that life is not always fair and that you cannot always live your life by principles.

Pauline

Pauline was nearing her forties and had never been unemployed before sustaining an accident at work. An electrical shock was discharged through her body, which was so powerful that it wiped her memory clean. One year after the injury, Pauline found herself in a rehabilitation unit, not knowing who she was, where she was or how she got there. Her husband and parents visited her there but, of course, she did not recognize them as such. She did not know she was married. Following the acute phase of her injury, there were few places that could treat her. Consequently Pauline was transferred to a rehabilitation unit at the other side of the country. The distance put between her and her family, she recalls, was not conducive to reconstructing forgotten relationships.

Pauline never returned to her employer and although she would have every right to be angry with her circumstances, she has no strong feeling on the issue. She has no recollection of what she has lost. She accepts her situation with relative contentedness but does report trying to put everything back into one piece. Pauline has the intrinsic ability to recognize that she survived something which could have killed her, giving her an optimistic, 'grateful for the time she does have with her children,' outlook on life. She wants to make life as liveable as possible.

Pauline's husband, she informed me, holds a slightly different outlook although not overly pessimistic. With three children dependent upon them, her husband gave up his job as a mechanic to try to pull the family through as best he could. She acknowledges the difficulty for her husband, and the one thing she would like to do is provide more parental support.

Pauline had been at home for years before she had the opportunity for vocational rehabilitation. Her one regret was that vocational rehabilitation had not been available earlier, then she would not have been stuck at home festering while her relationship with her family deteriorated. She has never returned to paid employment. She is currently undertaking repetitive factory work for experience and quite happy with it. She can undertake simple single tasks.

Peter

Peter acquired brain injury through an aneurysm causing right hemi-spheric damage. He now has no control or ability in the left-hand side of his body. Following the aneurysm, he was taken to the local accident and emergency unit. He reports that the hospital was not geared up to deal with his brain injury. He found himself in a single sex geriatric ward, surrounded by 80 and 90-year-old men. He remained here for three months, unable to make head or tail of his situation. He would like to see the health authorities geared up to deal better with younger people with an acquired head injury.

Peter's residual difficulties are mostly physical. The brain hemi-sphere designated to deal with the movements of the left side of the body is damaged, and consequently he has no control on that side of his body. There is also some subtle cognitive injury. For example, the concept of time seems to have been destroyed. He describes a few minutes seeming an eternity. Recent events appear to be a long time in the distant past. It also transpired that he had no concept of an accent on speech. My rather strong Glaswegian accent was not noticed or identifi-able. Nevertheless, Peter had not become depressed; he was grateful for having his life and determined to make the most of it.

Peter drew attention to a number of issues which were frustrating or made him angry. He dislikes the patronizing that happens to him, from both family/friends and from strangers. Ultimately he mourns the loss of his independence. He particularly becomes annoyed at the exuberant prices of aids and adaptations for disabled people which he feels is gross profiteering from a vulnerable and usually financially poor group. Our discussions took us on to the facilities available to disabled people. On the whole, he believes that there is a good pavement system within the UK for his electric cart, which he needs to get out and about. This is not always the case abroad. When travelling to another country, a lot more planning and research is needed before proceeding with your holiday. He is keen to acknowledge that the best place for a disabled person to get a taxi is in Leeds.

Peter rebels at being overprotected. He recalls on one occasion, while on holiday, he was nearly knocked over by a group of youths pushing past. The youths did not realize that he had a disability nor, he reflects, did they particularly care. While he was happy to let it go, his wife was not and took issue with the offenders. Peter felt that control of the situation had been taken from him and that he now had two issues to cope with, losing his balance and the ensuing argument with the youths.

Peter was eager to go back to his job. Nine months later he returned to his employer to undertake two hours' work per day. He had always enjoyed a positive relationship with his line manager, who unfortunately had moved on shortly before he had returned. Consequently when he returned to work, there was no support or real understanding of his problems. It became clear that he was not able to sustain his work duties.

He soon realized that someone else had been employed to undertake his job. They had a different job title but in effect it was his job. He confronted his employer but it was pointless, he felt. He had pinned a lot of hope on returning to employment, so recalls it being a bit of a body blow and possibly his lowest period. There were redundancies and he asked to be made redundant, but his employer insisted that he resign as unfit to carry out his work duties. He did. He had come and gone within two weeks.

Like many, Peter felt that he attempted a return to work too quickly. In retrospect he feels that two years would have been more appropriate. He is now three years post-injury and has been on a long-term rehabilitation programme and just about to start a paid job. He feels that this is just about the right period to return to employment. He is unable to undertake physical activity – even filing is not possible – but reception or computer/ administration work is something he has aspired to.

Jayne

Jayne worked as a hairdresser and was about 23 years of age when she acquired a brain injury. She was planning to start up her own hairdressing business in the very near future, just before she was involved in a road traffic accident which almost cost her her life. She was in a coma for three months. When she woke from the coma she hazily recalls her parents being present. It was a number of days before they told her that her sister had been killed in the accident. She recalled feeling how distant her happy childhood seemed to be. Her sense of guilt out-weighed by far any bitterness she felt at her own situation.

Jayne had no obvious cognitive problems. However, her speech was affected and the part of the brain that controlled motor movement was destroyed to the extent that she was a virtual tetraplegic. She felt caged and at 23 years of age, she could see her whole endless life stretching in front of her. Dreams of a family of her own had gone, as had grandchildren for her parents. She vowed to take one day at a time. What else was there for her to do?

She had started a vocational rehabilitation programme but she did not feel it was stretching her. Prior to that, she was at a special day centre for brain-injured people but felt that this reinforced her feeling of being disabled. She felt bored in the evening with nothing to do but watch television. Ideally she would return to her old job – all she ever wanted to do was to be a hairdresser. Perhaps she could do something with computers.

The one growing resentment that she did have was that none of her friends continued with their friendship. Of course, they turned up at the hospital with flowers and for the first few weeks would visit. Admittedly it must have been an unpleasant experience for them. She could not hold a conversation because of her speech difficulty and any communication would be peppered with emotional outbursts of guilt and sorrow at her injustice, but if there was any time in her life when she needed support, friendship and someone to listen, then this was it. She felt that had the situation been reversed, she would have remained loyal to them. She would have persevered. Now she feels that she does not need them. She can cope on her own.

Marie

Marie had not long left school and was working with a farrier as part of an employment training programme, when she was kicked in the head by a horse. The horse, she interjected, had quite a famous owner, but that was neither here nor there she acknowledges, just a fact she liked to recall. She was about 21 years of age at the time of the injury and mad keen on horses. She had been riding since childhood. As is often the case, she recalls nothing of the incident and finds it strange that family and friends seem to know more about it than she does. It is a growing frustration with her that everyone seems to be an expert on her life. She can recall waking up in hospital and wondering where on earth she was and how she got there. She has numerous physical injuries and severe cognitive impairment.

On the whole she found her treatment at hospital acceptable but was transferred to a rehabilitation unit without consultation, explanation or inclusion in the decision. On reflection, she felt they might have discussed this with her but she could not remember them doing so. She feels this lack of inclusion is generally characteristic of her experience since leaving hospital, including the vocational rehabilitation unit she is now in. Numerous appointments that have been made with specialists involved in her ongoing litigation for compensation are all at their convenience, not hers.

Her life has changed completely. She has lost any independence and much that was dear to her, sadly including the many friendships she had cultivated over the years. She is not sure what the future in terms of employment holds; it is on the back burner as she tries to establish her independence in other ways, but working on a farm would appeal to her.

She feels that she is ready to move on but the professionals involved in her care disagree, which she finds frustrating. 'It is my life, not theirs,' she retorted. She feels that the professionals in charge are given far too much power over her and treat her as a child, preventing her from improving. Given her situation, her family side with the professionals and will not disagree or challenge their opinion, which drives her to despair. She feels isolated and has adopted a 'me against the rest of the world' view of her situation. She feels that she needs to prove herself much more than others are ever expected to.

David

David was a father of three and working as a senior partner of a law firm when he was hit by a vehicle on his way to work. He incurred severe cognitive injury and damage to his vision. His wife was told to prepare herself for the worst. He recalls trying to get out of bed in the hospital but his legs being unable to support him. He recalls trying to escape from the hospital because he felt that there was nothing wrong with him. Fourteen years later, a period in which he has never sustained paid employment, he still does not want to admit to himself that there is anything wrong.

David's recollection of the hospital reads like a science fiction drama. He believed that he was being held capture in a foreign country. His language production and comprehension had been damaged and he could not understand the English language being spoken around him. The presence of Cyrillic script on a magazine in the hospital waiting room, a subject he had studied at university, helped to convince him that he was somewhere in the Balkans, when in fact he was in a London hospital. At one stage David was placed in a padded cell for his own safety. He was also sectioned under the Mental Health Act. His concern at the time was that being sectioned could destroy his ability to practise law.

David's personal and work life were both adversely affected. His partners in his firm asked him to resign his position. They felt that he was interfering with practice and that his situation upset staff members. He felt that it was his company, his files, his clients and his staff, and he had the right to participate in the day-to-day running of the firm. David co-owned the company and fought to retain his partnership as much as he could, but inevitably there was little he could do. He lost his firm. Not much later his wife divorced him and he had difficulty gaining access to his children.

A large compensation package and a lifetime trust fund meant that David did not have to be concerned about earning an income. However, this did not prevent the feelings of needing to make a contribution to society. He is fed up with being a passenger and feels guilty about not working. He wants to be useful. He would like to help people in need. He has tried for many jobs well within his capabilities but the rejection letters are hard to bear. He feels at the point of wanting to give up. He feels that he is drifting without direction, with no purpose in life. He acknowledges the need of a life project. Above all, he describes the aloneness of an individual with a brain injury or with any disability, what it feels like to be different. He is able to make acquaintances but not friends. He informs me that the only thing to look forward to is all in the past. Looking back he is warmed by the amount of friends he does have, who have retained their friendship with him, and the people from all over the world who, at the time of the injury, travelled to be with him.

For a long while he was embarrassed about his disability. He was conscious of monopolizing conversations and not giving opportunities for reciprocal communication. He felt he had to guard against taking over and was always looking for a cause to promote, but ever conscious not to patronize. He admits that, like many people with a characteristic that they dislike about themselves, he amplified the issue out of all proportion and made it more an issue to himself than anyone else. He is nevertheless fed up with being half of himself.

He has successfully returned to education as a mature student and undertaken research, but still not gained paid employment. He does not know what to do next; he just wants a job. He suspects his lack of confidence, recent experience and poor stamina are the main issues. He cannot accept that he is unable to achieve some things and becomes angry with himself when unable to. He is hostile to the idea of being described as disabled and wary of playing on it for the advantages that it can bring. He bridles at being told he needs help. He feels outside of society. He may look normal but that is half the problem.

Three days after this interview and 14 years after the initial injury, David was offered and accepted a job with the Law Society.

Note

1   Quotes in this chapter are from clients whose identity will remain anonymous.

Reducing Risk

Reducing risk of brain injury does not usually fall within the remit of employment professionals but nevertheless it is a question often asked of us. Consequently it is worth concluding with a few words on prevention.

The modern approach to healthcare is prevention being better than cure and this is certainly a worthy ideal in relation to brain injury. In the case of actual trauma such as a blow to the head or a road traffic accident, then little can be done to prevent it. I would certainly recommend nevertheless abiding by the law in using seat belts, either avoiding dangerous sports or using safety equipment in such leisure activities and taking out insurance for loss of earnings. Some causes of acquired brain injury such as stroke can be minimized. High blood pressure is a major factor in a stroke for the working age population and should be taken seriously by anyone unfortunate enough to have this condition. High blood pressure can be increased by stress, which can be minimized by identifying where stress levels are raised and working towards reducing the stressors.

Most jobs have a degree of stress, either in the tasks required or in the office politics. Unfamiliar work environments are particularly stressful. Being employed below your level of ability or unemployed can be equally stressful, so avoiding stressful environments is not always the easy answer. It is, however, much better to take a less pivotal role within an organization than to incur further health problems due to work-related stress. As with so much of the successful management of returning brain-injured people to employment, obtaining a balance of challenging but not overstressful work activity is a good goal to aim for. Monitoring of stress levels where possible would be beneficial. Also exploring relaxation methods could be considered, including massage, hot bath, yoga, music, herbs, aromatherapy and a whole host of other techniques which are available.

Common Terms Associated with Brain Injury

Acalculia
Loss or reduction of the ability to undertake calculations following damage to the brain.

Acquired head injury
An injury acquired as a result of a traumatic insult to the brain. Interchangeable with acquired brain injury. This can be contrasted with a congenital disability which is present at birth.

Ageusia
Partial or total loss of taste.

Agraphia
Loss of ability to express ideas in written form.

Alexia
Loss of the ability to read following damage to the brain.

Anarithmetria
Inability to undertake mathematics following damage to the brain.

Aneurysm
A cerebral aneurysm is a bulge of a blood vessel within the brain. Rupture of the aneurysm will result in bleeding within the brain.

Anomia
Inability to recall the names of an object. Clients with this problem often can speak fluently but need to use other words to describe familiar objects.

Aphasia (expressive, receptive, global)
Loss of the ability to comprehend or communicate verbally following an acquired head injury.

Apraxia
The inability to carry out purposeful movement. It is a motor disorder in which movement is impaired. Verbal apraxia refers to difficulty in sequencing speech sounds but without corresponding muscle weakness.

Ataxia

A problem of muscle co-ordination not due to apraxia, weakness, rigidity, spasticity or sensory loss. It is caused by lesion of the cerebellum or basal ganglia. This problem can interfere with a person's ability to walk, talk, eat and perform other tasks.

ADHD

Attention Deficit Hyperactivity Disorder is a congenital brain disorder affecting children and adults. The main characteristics of the disorder are inattention, hyperactivity and impulsivity.

Attention deficit

Damage to skills related to attention-concentration, ignoring distractions and/or shifting attention fluidly. These deficits often occur following brain injury.

Bilateral symmetry

The ability to use both hands in relatively equal measure at a subconscious level. A client with orthopaedic injury following acquired brain injury can be capable of using both hands/arms but through a process of conditioning can become overreliant on one side.

Case manager

An individual employed to co-ordinate activities and to provide support to an individual who needs assistance following an acquired disability.

CAT scan

This stands for Computerized Axial Tomography and is an X-ray-type procedure in which information regarding the body's organs can be cross-sectioned in 3D images. This enables a clearer understanding to surgeons of damage that has occurred to the brain.

Circumlocution

Substituting other words or phrases for words that cannot be expressed.

Cognitive

Actions or functions of the brain such as memory, concentration or executive skill. Chemical and electrical impulses which are the energy source within the brain.

Cognitive therapy/rehabilitation

An organized approach to improving cognitive abilities and generalizing these abilities into real-life situations. The primary goal is to maximize each individual's level of functional independence.

Coma
A state of unconsciousness from which the client cannot be aroused. Unconsciousness may last from a few seconds to a few months or longer. Generally, the longer the coma, the more severe the brain injury and less favourable the outcome. People begin to emerge from their coma when they open their eyes, speak or begin to obey commands.

Competency exercise
An exercise that has been specifically designed to either assess an individual's competence in a task or to provide an opportunity to practise a skill as a means of rehabilitation.

Concussion
Loss of awareness and capability. Physiologic and/or anatomic disruption of connections between some nerve cells in the brain. This is a common result of a brain injury and can be either temporary or prolonged.

Confabulation
Verbalizations about people, places and events with no basis in reality. The client appears to 'fill in' gaps in memory with plausible facts.

Contusion
The result of an injury that bruises the brain or any part of the body.

Coup damage
Damage to the brain at the point of impact.

CRISP
Cognitive Rehabilitation Independant Speech Programme. A computerised programme that promotes improvement in speech following acquired speech disorders.

CT scan
Interchangeable with CAT scan.

Development disorder
A childhood neurological disorder.

Diplopia
Double vision.

Disinhibition
Inability to suppress (inhibit) impulsive behaviour, feelings and emotions.

Dysarthria
Difficulty in forming or speaking words because of weakness of muscles used in speaking. Speech is characterized by slurred, imprecise articulation. Tongue movements are usually laboured and the rate of speaking may be very slow.

Dysexecutive syndrome
Combination of cognitive problems affecting decision-making ability.

Dyslexia
Reading and writing disorder which can be acquired as a consequence of a brain injury.

Edema
Swelling of the brain as a result of injury.

Electroencephalogram (EEG)
A method of measuring electrical activity in the brain.

Executive skills
Higher cognitive skills involved in planning and decision making.

Frontal lobes
Situated at the front of the brain concentrating on execution of tasks and planning of events and the control of movement.

Gastrostomy tube
A tube inserted through a surgical opening into the stomach. It is used as a pathway for liquids, food or medication into the stomach, when the client is unable to take such substances by mouth.

Glasgow Coma Scale
A method used by the medical profession to ascertain and record consciousness and response levels following a traumatic injury or suspected injury to the brain.

Haematoma
Haematoma is the collection of blood in tissues or a space following rupture of a blood vessel. The collection of blood on the brain will damage cells leading to cognitive injury.

Hemianopia
A loss of half the area of the visual field brought about by acquired brain injury.

Hemiparesis
Weakness of one side of the body, generally resulting from injury to the opposite hemisphere of the brain.

Hydrocephalus
Enlargement of fluid-filled cavities in the brain. This is often associated with excessive amount of cerebral spinal fluid (CSF).

Magnetic resonance imaging (MRI)
Similar to a CAT scan but uses magnetic fields to produce a picture of brain tissue. MRI scans are more sensitive than CAT scans or X-rays for detecting many structural brain abnormalities.

Neurological assessment
Assessment undertaken by a psychologist to determine the extent of cognitive injury following an acquired head injury.

Neuropsychology
The branch of psychology that tests different specific components of cognition by examining abilities such as memory, visual perception, reaction time, general intelligence, executive functions and sensorimotor skills. The neuro-psychologist works with the other members of the rehabilitation team to devise specific remediation strategies for the client, as well as providing supportive counselling and education.

Nystagmus
Involuntary jerking of the eye following injury to the brain stem.

Occipital lobe
The occipital lobe is located at the back of the brain and is mainly responsible for visual perception.

Occupational psychologist
An occupational psychologist specializes in work-related issues. In relation to a brain- injured client they may be involved in their assessment, rehabilitation or reintegration into mainstream employment.

Paresis
Muscle weakness or reduced motor functions secondary to damage to the brain pathways which regulate motor movement.

Parietal lobe
The parietal lobe is located above the occipital lobe and its main functions are processing sensation and perception as well as the integration of sensory information.

Post-traumatic amnesia
A period of confusion following brain trauma. The person is unable to recall what happened a few hours or even minutes ago. Individuals with this form of amnesia are confused and disoriented about the day, time, where they are and sometimes who they are.

Post-traumatic epilepsy
The development of a seizure disorder following brain injury. This is a common phenomenon following brain injury in which the scrambling of electrical activity within the brain results in uncontrolled electrical discharge. The brain is more susceptible to epilepsy following an acquired brain injury due to the scarring that occurs.

Premorbid
Prior to the injury.

Proprioception
Proprioception is the brain's unconscious awareness of where its body parts are in space and time.

Rancho Los Amigos Scale
An eight-level scale that notes a person's level of recovery from Coma (Level 1) to Purposeful-Appropriate (Level 8), following traumatic brain injury.

Rehabilitation
The process of helping a person to achieve his or her maximum functional potential. The rehabilitation process can speed up the natural healing process and teach the individual new strategies to deal with returning to a normal life. Research has shown continued recovery for many years post-injury.

Rehabilitation team
A group of professionals who work together to help a client recover from head injury. Members of the team may include physician (neurologist, physiatrist), nurse, occupational psychologist, cognitive therapist, physical therapist, occupational therapist, speech therapist, recreational therapist, social worker and members from other clinical specialities.

Retrograde amnesia
A period of memory loss for events that occurred before a brain injury. After acquiring brain injury through a traumatic event such as a car accident, the individual involved usually has no memory of the accident or events immediately preceding it. This can be a particular problem if memory loss extends back for longer periods of time.

Severe closed head injury
Six or more hours of unconsciousness or an initial Glasgow Coma Scale score of 3 to 8. This typically results in significant physical and cognitive alterations, which require intensive and prolonged treatment and rehabilitation.

Temporal lobe
Part of the brain dealing with sound, language and memory.

Tracheotomy
An operation where an incision is made on the neck to open the windpipe if there is an obstruction in the airway. Scar left at the base of the neck is often a telltale sign of a severe injury hence severe brain injury.

Visual neglect
A disorder characterized by the failure to acknowledge or respond to information in part of the visual field.

Vocational rehabilitation
Structured training which supports an individual in returning to employment. Vocational rehabilitation can involve a number of therapeutic interventions and practical supported work experience.

References

Berglas, D. and Playfair, G.L. (1988) *A Question of Memory*. London: Jonathon Cape.

Flanagan, J.C (1954) 'The Critical Incident Technique.' *Psychological Bulletin 51*, 4, 327–358.

Kelly, G. (1955) *The Psychology of Personal Constructs*. New York: Norton.

Malia, K., Bewick, K., Raymond, M. and Bennett, T. (1997, 2002) *Brainwave-R: Cognitive Strategies and Techniques for Brain Injury Rehabilitation*. Austin, Texas: Pro Ed, Inc.

Salvendy, G. (1987) *Handbook of Human Factors*. New York: John Wiley.

Turner-Stokes, L. (1999) 'The effectiveness of rehabilitation: A critical evaluation of the evidence.' *Clinical Rehabilitation 13*, Supplement.

Further Reading

Cognitive injury

Boake, C., Freeland, J.C., Ringholz, G.M., Nance, M.L. and Edwards, K.E. (1995) 'Awareness of memory loss after severe closed head injury.' *Brain Injury 9*, 3, 273–283.

Crosson, B., Barco, P.P., Velozo, C.A. *et al.* (1989) 'Awareness and compensation in post-acute head injury rehabilitation.' *Journal of Head Trauma Research 4*, 46–54.

Fleming J.M., Strong, J. and Ashton, R. (1996) 'Self-awareness of deficits in adults with traumatic brain injury: How best to measure.' *Brain Injury 10*, 1, 1–15.

Lezak, M.D. (1995) *Neuropsychological Assessment* (Third edition). Oxford: Oxford University Press.

Malia, K.B. (1997) 'Insight after brain injury: What does it mean?' *The Journal of Cognitive Rehabilitation 15*, 3, 10–12.

Matarazz, J.D. and Herman, D.O. (1985) 'Clinical use of the WAIS-R: Base rates of difference between VIQ and PIQ in the WAIS-R standardisation sample.' In B.B. Wolman (ed) *Handbook of Intelligence: Theories, Measurements and Applications.* New York: John Wiley and Sons.

Nelson, H.E. and O'Connell, A. (1978) 'Dementia: The estimation of pre-morbid intelligence levels using the new adult reading test.' *Cortex 14*, 234–244.

Occupational techniques

Annet, J. and Duncan, K.D. (1967) 'Task analysis and training design.' *Occupational Psychology 41*, 211–221.

Kay, D. and Hinds, R. (2002) *A Practical Guide to Mentoring.* Oxford: How To Books.

Kirwan, B. and Ainsworth, L.K. (1992) *A Guide to Task Analysis.* London: Taylor and Francis.

Lewis, G. (2000) *The Mentoring Manager.* London: Prentice Hall.

McCormick, E.J. (1979) *Job Analysis: Methods and Applications.* New York: Amacon.

SHL Group plc (2001) *Guidelines for Best Practice in the Use of Job Analysis Techniques.*

Spencer, Lyle M. and Spencer, Signe M. (1993) *Competence at Work: Models for Superior Performance.* New York: John Wiley and Sons.

Index